Timeless Essays About Islam and its Doctrine

What It Includes and Why It Matters

Elaine Ellinger

www.poi-nps.com

Perspectives on Islam

Perspectives on Islam
Website: https://www.poi-nps.com/

Print ISBN: 978-1-0688760-1-1
Ebook ISBN: 978-1-0688760-3-5

Koran Chapter 8:
Surat Al-'Anfāl (The Spoils of War)

They ask you (O Muhammad) about the spoils of war. Say: "The spoils are for Allah and the Messenger." So fear Allah and adjust all matters of difference among you, and obey Allah and His Messenger (Muhammad), if you are believers. (Koran 8:1)

Narrated Abu Huraira:

Allah's Messenger [Mohammed] said, "Allah guarantees him who strives in His Cause and whose motivation for going out is nothing but Jihad in His Cause and belief in His Word, that He will admit him into Paradise (if martyred) or bring him back to his dwelling place, whence he has come out, with what he gains of reward and booty." (Sahih Bukhari, 3123)

CONTENTS

INTRODUCTION:

My interest in Islam developed after sharing a house with a Bahai refugee from the Iranian revolution in 1983. Over Christmas, we were the only two left in the house and celebrated the season together, cutting down a tree, decorating it and listening to carols on the radio.

I learned how he had come to Canada for safety because he and his friends had been tortured, and some had been killed, simply because they were Bahai. I couldn't imagine such a thing and had no understanding of Islam at the time.

Now I do.

PREFACE AND ACKNOWLEDGEMENTS

hy are these essays timeless you may ask? Because Islamic doctrine is considered 'perfect' and cannot be changed. Places and faces vary over time but the effect of sharia on non-Islamic countries tends to follow a recognizable pattern that is also predictable for those who have studied it.

There are many facets to sharia (the 'ordained way of Islam). The intention of this book is to present these facets in a way that removes some of the mystery and facilitates understanding. While certain topics may interest the reader more than others, I do highly recommend reading the first three essays before reading the rest. They provide the necessary groundwork to correctly assess the significance of Islamic doctrine today, and will make it very easy to follow what is written in the remainder of the book.

This is not a history book, it doesn't delve deeply into any particular aspect of Islam, for the most part it's an overview to show the scope of a belief system that is rapidly spreading around the globe. It is spreading rapidly because of lack of knowledge on the part of host countries, whose leaders rely on advice (often provided by proponents of Islam) rather than learning about the doctrine from original sources for themselves.

For that reason the final two essays in this book are: 1. Sharia in a Nutshell and 2. Solutions. There are simple ways to protect human rights in non-Islamic states from the discrimination and brutality of sharia but first it is essential that authorities know for themselves what sharia is, and then adhere to the principles found in the Universal Declaration of Human Rights to resist it.

I'll take this opportunity to thank all the many people I have worked and spoken with over the last few years in relation to this topic. In particular Robert Kerr, Diane Bederman, Deb Curtis, Scott Morgan, John Walsh, Alan Altany, Robert Bodisch, Patricia Ray, Marco Bumaguin, L&G, Clare Lopez, Helen and Min. And a big thank you to reviewers Steve Kirby and Robert Spencer. For those who cannot be named, you know who you are and your knowledge, comments, criticism, suggestions and constant support have been a wonderful help to me.

I also wish to thank personal friends who have stuck with me through thick and thin and most especially my husband, my safe harbour, purveyor of valuable feedback, and the love of my life, Ken.

CHAPTER ONE

WHO ARE THE EXPERTS ON ISLAM?

Maybe not who you'd expect...

A recent post on LinkedIn generated a lot of comments, a lot of opinions, but the only two experts on Islam that really matter are Allah and Mohammed. Every word in the Koran was uttered by Mohammed. If it is not from Allah and Mohammed, it is not Islam.

This is why the best source of knowledge on this subject is the foundational Islamic doctrine itself. Many people have tried reading the Koran and found it very confusing – partly because the Koran is not in chronological order but also because they don't know the complete and factual biography (Sira) of Mohammed who exemplifies the actions that believers are expected to follow (1).

In addition, the story of Mohammed in Mecca, is very different from Mohammed after his migration to Medina. While Mohammed had only 150 followers after 13 years of non-violent preaching in Mecca, after his migration to Medina, and there becoming a military leader and politician, Islam grew to encompass the entire Arabian peninsula in only 9 years (2). This was accomplished after Mohammed adopted jihad as a tactic. In fact, Chapter 8 of the Koran is named Al-Anfal – 'The Spoils of War.'

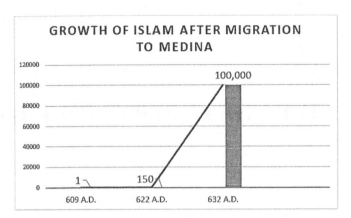

GROWTH OF ISLAM AFTER MIGRATION TO MEDINA

Several times in history, rulers of Islamic states have attempted to make their country more secular. A good example is Iran. The Iranian revolution ended that in 1979 and Sharia – the 'ordained way' of Islam found in the Koran and Hadith (stories and traditions about Mohammed) – was once again strictly enforced. This is called the 'gravity' of Mohammed, the return to the primary doctrine and his example (3).

Question: So why would non-Muslims want to learn about Islamic foundational doctrine anyway?

Answer: because more than half of it concerns them and as such, it is political.

- "Narrated Abu Huraira: A man came to Allah's Messenger and said, "Instruct me as to such a deed as equals Jihad (in reward)." Mohammed replied, "I do not find such a deed..." (Bukhari 2785)

It is only by knowing the life of Mohammed, that it is possible to understand Islam and its goal.

Check the sources for yourself. Study the doctrine...

Sources:

(1) Guillaume, Alfred. 'The Life of Muhammad: a Translation of Ishaq's Sirat Rasul Allah' (p.109-687) Oxford University Press, 1967 https://archive.org/details/GuillaumeATheLifeOfMuhammad/page/n3/mode/2up

(2) Military expeditions of Mohammed: https://en.wikipedia.org/wiki/List_of_expeditions_of_Muhammad

(3) Koran instructions to follow Mohammed: https://www.cspii.org/learn-political-islam/methodology/statistical-analysis-political-islam/number-times-koran-commands-muslims-imitate-mohammed/

RELEVANT DOCTRINE:

Koran 8:55 https://legacy.quran.com/8/55

Koran 33:61 https://legacy.quran.com/33/61

Hadith (Muslim 1767a) https://sunnah.com/muslim:1767a

Hadith (Bukhari 6098) https://sunnah.com/bukhari:6098

Hadith (Bukhari 3167) https://sunnah.com/bukhari:3167

Hadith (Bukhari 2785) https://sunnah.com/bukhari:2785

CHAPTER TWO

CAN ISLAM BE MODERNIZED?

For non-Islamic countries, there is another option

In non-Islamic countries, there are Muslims who say that Islam should be reformed and they often gain support from outside the Islamic community (1). This comes from conflating people with doctrine – the people are nice, therefore the doctrine (Koran and Hadith of Mohammed) can be made so.

Regarding the Koran, it has been suggested that only the earlier verses, intolerant towards unbelievers but not violent, should be retained, but on this point the Koran is clear: The later verse is better or stronger than the earlier one:

- Koran 2:106 Whatever a Verse (revelation) do We abrogate or cause to be forgotten, We bring a better one or similar to it. Know you not that Allah is able to do all things?

It has also been suggested that the Hadith (traditions and practices) of Mohammed could be revised or removed. But revising the life story of a dead man is not possible, and it is Allah who sent Mohammed with guidance and Islam to make it 'victorious over all other religions' (Koran 61:9). Even the five pillars of Islam rely on his example.

There are only two experts we can look to for answers that will be accepted by the entire Islamic community – the Koran and Mohammed. Here's what they say:

- The Koran is perfect (Koran 2:2)

- Mohammed is an excellent pattern to follow (Koran 33:21)

- Whoever changes his religion, then kill him' (Bukhari 6922)

- "The best talk is Allah's Book (Qur'an), and the best guidance is the guidance of Muhammad." (Bukhari 6098)

- Allah will not accept any fasting, prayer, charity, Hajj, 'Umrah, Jihad, or any other obligatory or voluntary action from a person who follows innovation (Ibn Majah 49)

Removing all reference to unbelievers in the Koran (64%) and jihad would leave little text (2).

- No follower will say that Allah and Mohammed were wrong

- Anything that contradicts them – is not truth in Islam

- To remove over half the text means to create a new one, not to edit the old one

- There are no authorities to oversee such a process

- The final arbiters of Islam are Mohammed and Allah, so who will confirm reformed texts?

- What would-be reformers and non-believers dislike in Islam is the tool for its success

- The process of jihad has been successfully and continuously practiced for 1400 years as an essential component in the growth of Islam.

In addition, Islam has a built in fail-safe to prevent reform. Mohammed said: "Allah will raise for this community at the end of every hundred years the one who will renovate its religion for it." (Dawud 4291) This is intended as a factory reset, to remove any deviation or innovation such as those being proposed by reformers (3).

Logically, for adherents, reform will have to come from within, but how is it possible to reform texts that cannot be changed, questioned or criticized? In Islamic countries even a Twitter/X post can result in prison or death (4). There is no satisfactory solution to this conundrum.

There is another option:

For non-Islamic countries, discovering ways to mitigate the negative aspects of Islam lies with education and full disclosure of the doctrine from the standpoint of the unbeliever. An option that has never been tried but has much to recommend it.

This is a peaceful, practical and realistic strategy for reform that unbelievers can manage for themselves, be certain of the content, and begin without delay. Individually or collectively, all that is required is the doctrine and the will to study it.

Sources:

(1) Douglas Williams, Christine "The Challenge of Modernizing Islam – Reformers Speak Out and the Obstacles They Face" 2017 Encounter Books Pub.

(2) Statistical analysis:
https://www.cspii.org/learn-political-islam/articles/statistical-islam/

(3) Islam Q&A:
https://islamqa.info/en/answers/153535/the-hadith-at-the-beginning-of-every

-century-allah-will-send-to-this-ummah-someone-who-will-renew-its-religious
-understanding

(4) News:
https://www.theguardian.com/world/2022/aug/16/saudi-woman-given-34-year-prison-sentence-for-using-twitter

RELEVANT DOCTRINE:

Koran 2:106 https://legacy.quran.com/2/106

Koran 2:2 https://legacy.quran.com/2/2

Koran 8:39 https://legacy.quran.com/8/39

Koran 9:60 https://legacy.quran.com/9/60

Koran 33:21 https://legacy.quran.com/33/21

Koran 61:9-11 https://legacy.quran.com/61/9-11

Hadith (Bukhari 6922) https://sunnah.com/bukhari:6922

Hadith (Muslim 523e) https://sunnah.com/muslim:523e

Hadith (Muslim 867a) https://sunnah.com/muslim:867a

Hadith (Bukhari 6584) https://sunnah.com/bukhari:6584

Hadith (Ibn Majah 3) https://sunnah.com/ibnmajah:3

Hadith (Ibn Majah 14) https://sunnah.com/ibnmajah:14

Hadith (Nasa'i 1578) https://sunnah.com/nasai:1578

Hadith (Tirmidhi 1432) https://sunnah.com/tirmidhi:1432

Hadith (Muslim https://sunnah.com/muslim:2889a

Hadith (Dawud 4291) https://sunnah.com/abudawud:4291

Hadith (Ibn Majah 49) https://sunnah.com/ibnmajah:49

CHAPTER THREE

HOW TO DO YOUR OWN RESEARCH

Islamic doctrine – what does it really say?

P eople are often confused by what they read or hear about Islamic doctrine and don't know what to believe. There is a solution. Learn how to research Islamic texts for yourself and not rely on others for information. Authentic foundational doctrine is best.

The primary resources used by Islamic scholars are the Koran and the Hadith of Mohammed. The example of Mohammed (his 'sunnah') is extremely important, without it, even the five pillars of Islam cannot be properly practiced.

Mohammed can be found in the Hadith collections (stories and traditions about Mohammed) and the Sira (Mohammed's biography). Together the Koran and Sunna provide the guidance for sharia – Islamic law, what to do and how to do it.

There are several Koran and Hadith search engines. The two examples below were chosen because the first includes several translations of the Koran, with the Arabic, and easily provides as much context as the reader wants.

The second search engine includes many Hadith including the 'six authentic' collections studied by many Islamic scholars: Bukhari, Muslim, Dawud, Tirmidhi, al-Nasa'i, Ibn Majah. You will find frequent references to these hadith collections throughout this book.

Hadith quality is graded, the best are 'sahih'. It may be useful to know that not all hadith have been translated. This includes important collections such as Musnad Ahmad (only 4% translated). Evidence of these hadith can be found in other sources such as 'Reliance of the Traveller' a handbook of sharia and the 'tafsir', commentaries about the Koran.

There are also three websites that are repositories of such data. These resources have already compiled many Koranic verses and hadith under listed topics such as: women, jihad, non-Muslim (Kafir) etc.

For anyone setting out to do their own research I recommend obtaining, or downloading the Sira 'Life of Mohammed', and the sharia manual 'Reliance of the Traveller', to a file on your computer and bookmarking the search engine websites for the Koran and Hadith in the bookmarks bar of your browser.

Data Sources:

Koran:
https://legacy.quran.com/
(I recommend the Hilali/Khan translation with commentary)

Hadith:
https://sunnah.com/

Sira:
Guillaume, Alfred. 'The Life of Muhammad, a Translation of Ibn Ishaq's Sirat Rasul Allah' Oxford University Press, 1967 *The first, and arguably the best, biography of Mohammed. 8thc.
https://archive.org/details/relianceofthetravellertheclassicmanualofislamicsacredlaw

Sharia manual (ROT): Reliance of the Traveller, Nuh Ha Mim Keller, Amana Publications 2015 (ROT) https://archive.org/details/relianceofthe travellertheclassicmanualofislamicsacredlaw

* Sharia is the ordained way of the Koran and Sunna of Mohammed (Koran 45:18), the teachings and example therein. The handbook is only for convenience, to look up specific situations without having to search through the Koran and Hadith.

Data Repositories (websites):

Perspectives on Islam: Provides links to all the above on the home page with a tutorial video, and a 'resource' page listing books, papers and videos examining the many facets of Islam from the perspective of the non-Muslim: https://www.poi-nps.com/

CSPII see 'research' in right sidebar: https://www.cspii.org/learn-political-islam/methodology/

Religion of Peace Koran subject index: https://thereligionofpeace.com/pages/quran/index.aspx

NOTES:

It is sometimes said that a Koran verse or hadith has been 'misinterpreted', and yes, the terminology does take some getting used to – for example – a sex slave will be referred to in the doctrine as 'what your right hand possesses'. However, this argument is 14 centuries old – most people were illiterate, and there were no books. If Mohammed's followers had questions, they were told to ask those who had memorized parts of the Koran or Hadith: 'Ask those who recall if you know not' (Koran 16:43)

Also, Islamic foundational doctrine was specifically forbidden to the non-Muslim until recently:

- "When one fears ...that a non-Muslim may touch it [the Koran], or that it may come into contact with some filth, then one must pick it up if there is no safe place for it..." (ROT e8.3).

But today, when 80% of the world's Muslims do not speak Arabic, it is necessarily translated for sale in many languages. The doctrine is available as are excellent translations by qualified scholars. If you are reading this, you don't need someone else to tell you what it says.

What is important, is that translations be consistent with the authentic history of the life of Mohammed – for example the Sira by Ibn Ishaq and the Hadith – rather than a softened version that is not accurate. Good translations of the Koran include Hilali/Khan, Pickthall, Spencer, Yusef Ali, Sahih International.

Be aware that there are many examples where trusted institutions, even school-books and museums, print and display inaccurate information – it is best to do the research for yourself so you won't be led astray.

TUTORIAL VIDEO – 'Easy Steps to Researching Islamic Doctrine': https://rumble.com/v41aj2b-researching-islamic-doctrine-tutorial.html

CHAPTER FOUR

ISLAMOPHOBIA...

Says who? And why do they say it?

Phobia – definition: an irrational fear. Islamophobia? This word, in its essence, denies the lived experience of the many people seeking refuge in non-Islamic countries owing to real, not imagined, fear for their lives and property, non-Muslims, Muslim apostates and homosexuals alike (1).

It is interesting to note that the word Islamophobia is not recorded in the 1995 edition of the Oxford dictionary yet as of May 2024, there are 3,352 Wikipedia pages describing Islamophobia in virtually every country of the world and language spoken – except those countries which are already Islamic (2).

The Organization of Islamic Co-operation (OIC), with 57 member states, has the largest voting block at the U.N. and publishes 'Islamophobia' reports on an annual basis. There is no shortage of financing for such reports and consequently there are many others to choose from – including from non-Islamic governments and academia (3)(4).

Such a proliferation of documentation suggests that the only way to escape the label is to become an Islamic State – one has to ask, is that the goal, and is it worth it? (5)

What is the experience for refugees once they have arrived in non-Islamic countries? At a recent conference of Coptic Christians in the U.S., one of the witnesses felt compelled to hide his identity while speaking for fear of retaliation against himself, his family, and friends still living in Sudan (6)(7).

In too many countries to list, Islam for many is a real and ever present threat. In November 2021, a Toronto student event featuring Nobel Peace Prize winner, and author Nadia Murad, who was captured and 'plunged into sexual slavery as a teen,' was cancelled by the school board because 'the book would be offensive to Muslims and "foster Islamophobia"' - wrongly conflating Muslims and Islam. Thus, the voice of those who have suffered is silenced, so too are the voices of those who wish to speak about it. In this way, non-Islamic countries de facto enforce blasphemy laws (8).

Whether through fear of being labelled an Islamophobe, or through the loss of life and home, the net effect is the same – the expanding influence of sharia around the globe, and lack of resistance from non-Islamic countries:

- The taking of slaves, "...We have made lawful to you your wives to whom you have given their due compensation and those **your right hand possesses** from what Allah has returned to you [**of captives**]..." (Koran 33:50)

- Captives for ransom, "So when you meet those who disbelieve [in battle], strike [their] necks until, when you have inflicted slaughter upon them, then secure their bonds, and either [confer] favor afterwards **or ransom** [them] until the war lays down its burdens. ..."(Koran 47:4)

- Property, "...Have they not seen that We set upon the land, reducing it from its borders? And Allah decides; there is no adjuster of His decision...." (Koran 13:41)

- Booty, "...I wish I had been with them; then I would have achieved a great success (a good share of booty). ..." (Koran 4:73)

- And lives, "...I will cast terror into the hearts of those who disbelieved, so strike [them] upon the necks and strike from them every finger-tip." (Koran 8:12)

All are found in the foundational Islamic doctrine and are therefore sacrosanct. Is it not time for those of us living in the relative safety of non-Islamic countries, to shed our fears, find our voice, and learn to speak factually about Islam on behalf of those who cannot speak for themselves?

Sources:

(1) Jihad attacks:
https://thereligionofpeace.com/attacks/attacks.aspx?Yr=Last30

(2) Wikipedia Islamophobia:
https://en.wikipedia.org/w/index.php?fulltext=1&search=islamophobia&title=Special%3ASearch&ns0=1

(3) Government of Canada – Canadian Heritage News Release July 22, 2021
https://www.canada.ca/en/canadian-heritage/news/2021/07/the-government-of-canada-concludes-national-summit-on-islamophobia.html

(4) Georgetown University:
https://bridge.georgetown.edu/

(5) Canada News:
https://nationalpost.com/opinion/barbara-kay-liberals-left-reeling-by-clear-rational-criticisms-of-m-103

(6) U.S. Conference:
https://www.youtube.com/watch?v=bKm7bOq_aZ4&t=1s

(7) Africa News:
https://www.aciafrica.org/news/8071/over-50000-christians-killed-in-nigeria-since-2009-islamic-uprising-intersociety-report

(8) Canada News:
ttps://web.archive.org/web/20220429005649/https://nypost.com/2021/11/27/toronto-school-cancels-isis-survivor-event-with-nadia-murad/

EDUCATIONAL VIDEO:
https://www.youtube.com/watch?v=xZsMDOeUnBg&t=2s

RELEVANT DOCTRINE:

Koran 8:12 https://legacy.quran.com/8/12

Koran 2:221 https://legacy.quran.com/2/221

Koran 8:69 https://legacy.quran.com/8/69

Koran 13:41 https://legacy.quran.com/13/41

Koran 47:4 https://legacy.quran.com/47/4

Koran 57:15 https://legacy.quran.com/57/15

Bukhari 3053 https://sunnah.com/bukhari:3053

CHAPTER FIVE

IS THE CHARTER OF MEDINA SIGNIFICANT TODAY?

And why was it cited at a counter-terrorism lecture?

In the question period following a recent counter-terrorism lecture, it was mentioned that the hostility towards Jews found in Islamic primary doctrine began after Mohammed's migration from Mecca to Medina where there were three long-established Jewish tribes.

One of the lecture participants then cited the 'Charter of Medina' as an example of co-operation between Mohammed and the Jews, so it is useful to know what that Covenant consisted of.

The Covenant of Medina set out "reciprocal obligations" and for the first time described Mohammed's "believers and Muslims" as "one community (umma) to the exclusion of all men." That a "believer shall not slay a believer for the sake of an unbeliever, nor shall he aid an unbeliever against a believer." That "believers are friends one to the other to the exclusion of outsiders" and that "no polytheist shall intervene against a believer." Whenever there were differences about a matter they had to be "referred to God and to Muhammad." "The close friends of the Jews are as themselves. None of them shall go out to war save with the permission of Muhammad" (1).

Within five years of Mohammed's migration to Medina, all members of the three Jewish tribes had either accepted Islam, been exiled or killed (2).

The migration (hijra) to Medina is significant, marking the beginning of the Islamic calendar and a change of tactics to include 'fighting in the cause of Allah' – jihad – in the spread of Islam. Mohammed himself personally participated in 27 such battles (3).

The Koran frequently (4) reminds readers to look to Mohammed's example for guidance:

- "...There has certainly been for you in the Messenger of Allah an excellent pattern for anyone whose hope is in Allah and the Last Day..." (Koran 33:21)

Sources:

(1) Guillaume, Alfred. 'The Life of Muhammad: a Translation of Ishaq's Sirat Rasul Allah' (p. 231-232), Oxford University Press, 1982
https://archive.org/details/GuillaumeATheLifeOfMuhammad/page/n3/mode/2up

(2) Ibid (p. 281, 363, 437, 461-66)

(3) Ibid (p. 659).

(4) List of Koranic verses recommending Mohammed as a role model:
https://cspi-web-media.ams3.cdn.digitaloceanspaces.com/documents/The_Sunna_of_Mohammed.pd

RELEVANT DOCTRINE:

Koran Chapter 59 (Exile) https://legacy.quran.com/59

Koran 3:12 https://legacy.quran.com/3/12-13

Koran 3:28 https://legacy.quran.com/3/28

Koran 3:12 https://legacy.quran.com/3/12-13

Koran 33:26-27 https://legacy.quran.com/33/26-27

Koran 9:29 https://legacy.quran.com/9/29

Hadith Muslim 1765 https://sunnah.com/muslim:1765

Hadith Bukhari 3152 https://sunnah.com/bukhari:3152

Hadith Bukhari 7157 https://sunnah.com/bukhari:7157

CHAPTER SIX

WHAT HAPPENS WHEN DECLARATIONS OF HUMAN RIGHTS CONFLICT?

And U.N. member states subscribe to both of them...

Another document worthy of study, and directly related to the Charter of Medina, is the 2021 Cairo Declaration of the Organization of Islamic Cooperation on Human Rights (1). This document is subscribed to by the 57 states of the Organization of Islamic Cooperation (OIC). Fifty-six of these states are also members of the United Nations which adopted the Universal Declaration of Human Rights in 1948 (2).

Excerpts from the 2021 Cairo Declaration:

1. The Member States of the OIC recognize 'Islam as viceregent of Allah on Earth' proceeding from a belief in human rights and from a 'commitment to ensuring and protecting these rights as safeguarded *by the teachings of Islam*'

2. 'Aiming to contribute to the efforts of mankind to assert human rights... *in accordance with the Islamic values and principles*'

3. 'Cognizant of their virtuous and time-honored mores, credited with the oldest human rights pact in Islam; the Charter of Medina, [and] the last sermon of the Prophet Mohamed... should *underpin the conception of human rights*' (3).

The Declaration then sets out the 'Articles' which are agreed to: '*Without prejudice to the principles of Islam...*' Article 25 again states 'Everyone has the right to exercise and enjoy the rights and freedoms set out in the present declaration, *without prejudice to the principles of Islam...*'

DISCUSSION:

In the Cairo Declaration, the first pact referred to is the 'Charter of Medina', which declares that "believers and Muslims" are "one community (umma) to the exclusion of all men." That a "believer shall not slay a believer for the sake of an unbeliever, nor shall he aid an unbeliever against a believer." That "believers are friends one to the other to the exclusion of outsiders.

The second pact, 'the last sermon of Mohammed', regarding wives states 'God allows you to... beat them but not with severity." And urges men to 'Lay injunctions on women kindly, for they are prisoners with you having no control of their persons." Listeners are reminded that they have been left with, and to hold fast to, "the book of God [Koran} and the practice of His prophet [Mohammed]."

This is the 'ordained way' of sharia. (Koran 45:18)

While the 1990 Cairo Declaration explicitly stated:

- Article 24: "All rights and freedoms stipulated in this Declaration are subject to the Islamic Shari'ah"

- Article 25: "The Islamic Shari'ah is the only source of reference for the explanation or clarification of any of the articles in this Declaration"

...and the 2021 revision does not; it is nevertheless necessary to be aware of the importance, and carefully study, the historical documents 'underpinning' the current Cairo Declaration and recognize that this is still, in fact, sharia.

By comparison, and NOT preceded by the caveat 'without prejudice', the Universal Declaration of Human Rights states in Article 1 that "All human beings are born free and equal in dignity and rights".

Fourteen centuries later, the 'Charter' and 'Final Sermon', are still of such vital importance to Islam that they are enshrined in the OIC's current declaration of Human Rights.

CONCLUSION:

It is clear from the foregoing that the Cairo Declaration of Human Rights and the Universal Declaration of Human Rights represent two very different and divergent points of view.

All human beings are born free and equal or they are not, these are two positions that cannot be reconciled. Nevertheless, OIC members who have subscribed to both declarations are able to participate in committees, and vote on U.N. resolutions, that affect all people - not just those of the OIC.

As a consequence, and with regard to many U.N. decisions, citizens of non-OIC countries may wish to ask themselves and their representatives - which Declaration of Human Rights carries the most weight, and how can we be sure?

Sources:

(1) Cairo Declaration of Human Rights:
https://www.oic-oci.org/upload/pages/conventions/en/CDHRI_2021_ENG.pdf

(2) Universal Declaration of Human Rights: Universal Declaration of Human Rights:
https://www.ohchr.org/sites/default/files/UDHR/Documents/UDHR_Translations/eng.pdf

(3) Guillaume, Alfred. 'The Life of Muhammad: a Translation of Ishaq's Sirat Rasul Allah' (p. 231-32, 650-51,). Oxford University Press, 1982 (ibn Ishaq 8th c.)
https://archive.org/details/GuillaumeATheLifeOfMuhammad/page/n3/mode/2up

RELEVANT DOCTRINE:

Koran 4:34 https://legacy.quran.com/4/34

Koran 45:18 https://legacy.quran.com/45/18

Koran 48:29 https://legacy.quran.com/48/29

Hadith (Dawud 1905) https://sunnah.com/abudawud:1905

Chapter Seven

The Influencers

Who are they anyway?

Trending. A 25 second video 'short' of a well known influencer describing his conversion to Islam. Another 15 seconds would have revealed his remark that he didn't actually know much about Islam - but that was cut off (1)(2). After all, how credible is an influencer who's just admitted to a lack of knowledge concerning the product he's promoting?

- Mohammed said "If ten scholars of the Jews would follow me, no Jew would be left upon the surface of the earth who would not embrace Islam." (Muslim 2793)

I frequently recommend to people that they learn about Islamic doctrine themselves, from foundational sources. The reason for this is twofold:

1. INSTITUTIONAL CAPTURE:

Long established educational institutions such as museums and schools, or other influencers such as entertainers, banks and politicians can no longer be trusted as purveyors of truth regarding Islam.

A Few Examples:

The Islamic Museum of Australia displays a large wall plaque providing a short biography of Mohammed. The biography extols Mohammed's virtues and states that he vastly improved the lives of women – but makes no mention of violent jihad, sex slaves and multiple wives, or that he personally took part in 27 of a minimum 65 military expeditions (3)(4).

School books: a study investigating how Islam is portrayed in school books concluded that the deficiencies are "uniquely concerning" and that "Islamic activists use multiculturalism… to advance and justify the makeover of Islam-related textbook content" (5).

In light of recent demonstrations at non-Islamic Universities supporting the actions of what is a designated terrorist organization in many countries, it's worth noting that donations from Qatar and Saudi Arabia, to Penn and Harvard schools in the U.S., topped 19 million in the last 2 years alone (6). Consider that the 'Muslim Student Association' was established in 1963 with the assistance of the Muslim Brotherhood (7). And that "The Muslim Brotherhood Project' documented as evidence in the 'Holy Land Foundation Trial' (8) was set in motion over four decades ago:

- "Point of Departure 11: To adopt the Palestinian cause as part of a worldwide Islamic plan, with the policy plan and by means of jihad, since *it acts as the keystone of the renaissance of the Arab world today* (9)

Concerning the economy, the rise of Islamic finance in recent decades has been described as *'a politically-driven Islamist invention masked in religious idiom'* (10). Founded in Luxembourg in 1978, the Islamic Banking System (now called the Islamic Banking House) can be found throughout the non-Islamic world. Even though the European Council for Fatwa and Research recommended that Muslims utilize Islamic finance when it is available, it also stated that it is permissible to trade with usury and other contracts in non-Islamic countries utilizing the principle of 'darura' – necessity makes the forbidden possible. And of course this is what would be expected in a non-Islamic country and this was the practice until recent times.

However, once authorities accommodate demands for sharia finance, the argument of 'darura' no longer applies and Muslims will be pressured to purchase the Islamic alternative. *Now a theological imperative has been created where there was none before.* This facilitates the Islamization of non-Islamic economies while simultaneously contributing to the financing of 'zakat' the Islamic tax which also funds jihad (Koran 9:60).

In 2007 there were already several major U.K. institutions involved in Sharia Finance, all with Sharia Boards comprised of Islamic experts linked to: The Muslim Brotherhood, Saudi Wahhabi-Salafism, the Pakistani Deoband movement and Jama'at-i-Islami and its network (11). Today, Islamic finance is available in an ever expanding list of non-Islamic countries – countries that are ill-equipped to address any legal issues that arise without calling on Islamic experts for advice about sharia (12).

2. SHARIA:

Unlike other belief systems, deception is sanctioned in Islam in certain cases and to varying degrees.

From 'Reliance of the Traveller, a Classic Manual of Islamic Sacred Law' – recommended by al Azhar University (13):

- "Scholars say that there is no harm in giving a misleading impression if required by an interest countenanced by Sacred Law..."(r10.3)

- Outright lying is permissible in 3 cases: "war, settling disagreements, and a man talking with his wife or she with him." (r8.2) In fact Mohammed said "War is deceit" (Bukhari 3030)

- Deception, such as omitting important information to leave an erroneous impression, is preferable but "it is permissible to lie when the goal is permissible... obligatory if the goal is obligatory." "But it is religiously more precautionary in all such cases to employ words that give a misleading impression..."(r8.2)

Mohammed said "If you embrace Islam, you will be safe. You should know that the earth belongs to Allah and His Apostle, and I want to expel you from this land...." (Bukhari 3167)

What can be done about it? Knowledge is key.

Sources:

(1) Influencer video short version
https://youtube.com/shorts/vm1jJbsL7Zk?feature=share

(2) Influencer video complete version (watch 13:45 – 14:30)
https://www.youtube.com/watch?v=diqgTxR99JE&t=4s

(3) Islamic Museum:
https://www.google.com/local/place/fid/0x6ad644a31b5a4b53:0x7e105520bb
a1e07e/photosphere?iu=https://lh5.googleusercontent.com/p/AF1QipNnT7q
s1SemZZ7yKHHk7aPo6iSYaIW9u0LRTIa6%3Dw160-h106-k-no-pi0.050250
623-ya199.465-ro0.12615247-fo100&ik=CAoSLEFGMVFpcE5uVDdxczFTZ
W1aWjd5S0hIazdhUG82aVNZYUlXOXUwTFJUSWE2

(4) Guillaume, Alfred. 'The Life of Muhammad: a Translation of Ishaq's Sirat Rasul Allah'. #973, Oxford University Press, 1967
https://archive.org/details/history-ibn-ishaq-sirat-rasul-allah-the-life-of-muham
mad/page/n7/mode/2up

(5) School books:
https://files.eric.ed.gov/fulltext/ED501724.pdf

(6) University sponsors:
https://www.washingtonexaminer.com/news/2436243/penn-and-harvard-rake
d-in-19-7-million-from-qatar-and-saudi-arabia-in-last-two-years/

(7) Muslim Student Association:
https://en.wikipedia.org/wiki/Muslim_Students_Association

(8) U.S. Dept of Justice:
https://www.justice.gov/opa/pr/federal-judge-hands-downs-sentences-holy-lan
d-foundation-case

(9) Muslim Brotherhood 'Project' p.16 https://www.investigativeproject.org/d
ocuments/misc/687.pdf

(10) Sookhdeo, Patrick 'Understanding Shari'a Finance – The Muslim Challenge
to Western Economics' (p.79) Isaac Publishing

(11) Ibid (p.73, 81, 84)

(12) Canada News: https://torontosun.com/opinion/columnists/fatah-shariah
-law-makes-a-comeback-in-ontario

(13) Sharia, Reliance of the Traveller (r8.2, r9.1, r10.2-3) Nuh Ha Mim Keller,
Amana Publications 2015
https://archive.org/details/relianceofthetravellertheclassicmanualofislamicsacre
dlaw

Educational Video: How to do your own research:
https://rumble.com/v41aj2b-researching-islamic-doctrine-tutorial.html

Educational Video: Did Islam improve the lives of women:
https://rumble.com/v44liw2-did-islam-improve-the-lives-of-women.html

Educational Video: The Use of Deception in Islam:
https://youtu.be/9eP8tnQEWf8

RELEVANT DOCTRINE:

Koran 3:28 https://legacy.quran.com/3/28

Koran 66:2 https://legacy.quran.com/66/2

Koran 5:89 https://legacy.quran.com/5/89

Koran 9:123 https://legacy.quran.com/9/123

Koran 2:225 https://legacy.quran.com/2/225

Koran 9:1 https://legacy.quran.com/9/1

Hadith (Bukhari 3030) https://sunnah.com/bukhari:3030

Hadith (Bukhari 3941) https://sunnah.com/bukhari:3941

Hadith (Muslim 2793) https://sunnah.com/muslim:2793

Hadith (Bukhari 4037) https://sunnah.com/bukhari:4037

Hadith (Bukhari 2947) https://sunnah.com/bukhari:2947

Hadith (Tirmidhi 1927) https://sunnah.com/tirmidhi:1927

Hadith (Ibn Majah 225) https://sunnah.com/ibnmajah:225

Hadith (Bukhari 3167) https://sunnah.com/bukhari:3167

CHAPTER EIGHT

SEX SLAVES?

I was recently asked if it is true that in addition to his wives, Mohammed also kept sex slaves? According to Islamic foundational texts, this is true. While the doctrine limits the number of husbands to one, and the number of wives to four, in the case of Mohammed, the angel Gabriel revealed:

- "O Prophet! Lo! We have made lawful unto thee thy wives unto whom thou hast paid their dowries, **and those whom thy right hand possesseth [captives and slaves] of those whom Allah hath given thee as spoils of war**, and the daughters of thine uncle on the father's side and the daughters of thine aunts on the father's side, and the daughters of thine uncle on the mother's side and the daughters of thine aunts on the mother's side who emigrated with thee, and a believing woman if she give herself unto the Prophet and the Prophet desire to ask her in marriage - a privilege for thee only, not for the (rest of) believers - We are Aware of that which We enjoined upon them concerning their wives and those whom their right hands possess - that thou mayst be free from blame, for Allah is ever Forgiving, Merciful." (Koran 33:50)

Of more concern, is that the actions and instructions of Mohammed are repeatedly described in Islamic doctrine as setting an 'exalted standard' (Koran 68:4) to be followed – whether this is his example in Mecca, where Mohammed had only one wife for 25 years, or that of Medina, where he took many wives, concubines, and sex slaves as 'spoils of war' (1)(2)(3).

Although the latter is rarely spoken of in non-Islamic countries, both examples are sunnah (in accordance with the teaching of Islam) and therefore, sacrosanct. Reports of captured women being used as sex slaves by jihadis, or the common place kidnapping of young women and girls with forced conversion to Islam, continue to this very day but are rarely mentioned in the mainstream news.

Examples range from large scale Boko Haram raids on schools in Nigeria (4) to the targeted kidnapping of Coptic Christian women in Egypt (5) and Hindu women in Pakistan to be forcibly married and converted to Islam (6)(7)(8).

Slavery, in the foundational doctrine of Islam, is not a subject that is relegated to the annals of history. The information is there, and relevant today, for those who are willing to speak to it.

Sources:

(1) Guillaume, Alfred. 'The Life of Muhammad: a Translation of Ishaq's Sirat Rasul Allah' (p. 231-32, 650-51,). Oxford University Press, 1982 (ibn Ishaq 8th c.)
https://archive.org/details/GuillaumeATheLifeOfMuhammad/page/n3/mode/2up

(2) Kitab at-Tabaqat al-Kabir By Muhammad Ibn Sad 9c.(trans. Bewley 1995) Vol. 8 p. 39-118

(3) WikiIslam:
https://wikiislam.github.io/wiki/List_of_Muhammads_Wives_and_Concubines.html

(4) Australia news (Sept/23)
https://christiantoday.com.au/news/kidnapped-christian-schoolgirls-in-nigeria-converted-to-islam-in-video-released-by-boko-haram.html

(5) Ibrahim, Raymond (Egypt Aug/23)
https://www.copticsolidarity.org/2023/08/30/targeted-for-conversion-how-or
ganized-muslim-networks-prey-on-christian-women-in-egypt/?eType=EmailBl
astContent&eId=9ae4ed55-4278-4bc7-86b0-eb11e8cc8253

(6) Thomson, Mike BBC News (March/21)
https://www.bbc.com/news/stories-56337182

(7) India News (Sept/22)
https://www.indiatoday.in/world/story/hindu-woman-teenage-girls-abducted-f
orcibly-converted-pakistan-2004440-2022-09-25

(8) U.S. Magazine (June/22)
https://www.persecution.org/2022/07/04/reports-show-2000-women-girls-kid
napped-pakistan/

RELEVANT DOCTRINE:

Koran 23:5-6 https://legacy.quran.com/23/2-6

Koran 33:50 https://legacy.quran.com/33/50

Koran 68:4 https://legacy.quran.com/68/4

Bukhari 2229: https://sunnah.com/bukhari:2229

CHAPTER NINE

MOHAMMED WASN'T BLACK

And he had MANY slaves...

S etting the record straight. Mohammed was not black and slavery is far from over.

Indigenous people in several countries are being told that Islam is the 'natural religion of black people' – or some variation of that theme – and that they would be better served by converting to Islam. This myth was promulgated by the 'Nation of Islam' in the U.S. in the 1930s and attracted many followers, but with racial division being fostered at every turn, this story is making a comeback today (1)(2).

Mohammed was a light-skinned Arab and many hadith describe the remarkable whiteness of his leg, thigh, shanks, forearms, armpits, abdomen, cheeks, complexion and his 'elegant white colour' (Muslim 2340b); 'neither very white nor tawny.' (Bukhari 5900)

Islam is not a race and neither is it a colour.

Human beings in many countries are still being captured and then sold as slaves in Islamic states such as Libya (3), Yemen (4), Iraq (5), and Niger (6). And even though Saudi Arabia finally abolished slavery in 1962, and Oman in 1970, decades later many migrant workers describe exploitation reaching 'slavery-like conditions' (7).

How can this be?

The Koran is eternal, universal, and perfect and requires believers to follow the example of Mohammed 'And verily, you (O Muhammad) are on an exalted standard of character.' (Koran 68:4)

Mohammed had slaves, many slaves.

- "A man amongst us declared that his slave would be freed after his death. The Prophet [Mohammed] called for that slave and sold him. The slave died the same year." (Bukhari 2534)

People are often told that Mohammed and his followers released slaves – yes, sometimes, for the benefit of the person doing the releasing and only after the slave had converted to Islam. By converting to Islam, a slave would have the hope of being released if it in some way benefitted the 'owner' to expiate some 'wrong-doing' or if the slave could pay. (Muslim 1111e)

Freeing a slave was considered an act of charity, not justice, or a human right. For example, as a penalty, Mohammed "commanded the person (who) broke the fast in Ramadan to free a slave..." Or a slave might be released at the ''owner's' death in expectation of heavenly reward. (Muslim 1004a)

Captives taken in Mohammed's many battles were sometimes tortured, their wives and children taken as slaves. At Khaybar, Mohammed had one of the leaders tortured to death and his wife taken as a slave (8). She was very beautiful so Mohammed took Safiya as his own wife that very night. (Dawud 2998)

Colour has never been a barrier to who can be enslaved. Islamic slave-traders have sold not only Africans but also millions of white Europeans, from as far north as the Netherlands and even Iceland.

Jihadi slave raids by the Tatars alone into Poland, Ukraine and Russia between the 15th and 17th centuries numbered over 3 million and many died. "Often in chains", captives were marched to the slave markets "the old and infirm who will not fetch much as a sale, are given up to the Tatar youths either to be stoned, or thrown into the sea, or to be killed by any sort of death they might please" (9)(10)(11).

Slavery isn't over. Following the example of Mohammed permits it (12).

Sources:

EDUCATIONAL VIDEO: Mohammed wasn't black
https://www.youtube.com/watch?v=q2aSSiRi-3M&t=1s

(1) Pew Research:
https://www.pewresearch.org/short-reads/2019/01/17/black-muslims-account
-for-a-fifth-of-all-u-s-muslims-and-about-half-are-converts-to-islam/

(2) Oxford Bibliographies:
https://www.oxfordbibliographies.com/display/document/obo-978019539015
5/obo-9780195390155-0130.xml

(3) Libya slave trade:
https://www.usatoday.com/story/news/world/2017/11/23/slave-trade-libya-ou
trage-across-africa/891129001/

(4) Yemen:
https://en.wikipedia.org/wiki/Slavery_in_Yemen

(5) Iraq:
https://www.iraqinews.com/features/exclusive-isis-document-sets-prices-christi
an-yazidi-slaves/

(6) Slavery in Africa:
https://www.theguardian.com/global-development/2022/jun/28/child-sex-traff
icking-wahaya-girls-slavery-niger

(7) Human Rights Watch:
https://www.hrw.org/report/2004/07/13/bad-dreams/exploitation-and-abuse
-migrant-workers-saudi-arabia

(8) Guillaume, Alfred. 'The Life of Muhammad: a Translation of Ishaq's Sirat Rasul Allah' (#764). Oxford University Press, 1982 (ibn Ishaq 8th c.)
https://archive.org/details/GuillaumeATheLifeOfMuhammad/page/n3/mode/2up

(9) Webb, Simon "The Forgotten Slave Trade, the White European Slaves of Islam" Pen and Sword Books 2021

(10) The Legacy of Jihad (Bostom, Andrew MD ed) p 679-81 Prometheus Books 2005

(11) Ibrahim, Raymond 'Crucified Again, Exposing Islam's New War on Christians' Regnery Publishing 2013

(12) BBC News:
https://www.bbc.com/news/uk-england-south-yorkshire-61868863

RELEVANT DOCTRINE:

Koran 4:59 https://legacy.quran.com/4/59

Koran 16:71 https://legacy.quran.com/16/71

Koran 16:74-76 https://legacy.quran.com/16/74-76

Koran 4:24 https://legacy.quran.com/4/24

Koran 70:30 https://legacy.quran.com/70/30

Koran 23:6 https://legacy.quran.com/23/6

Koran 33:50 https://legacy.quran.com/33/50

Hadith (Bukhari 1365g) https://sunnah.com/muslim:1365g

Hadith (Muslim 495a) https://sunnah.com/muslim:495a

Hadith (Bukhari 7236) https://sunnah.com/bukhari:7236

Hadith (Muslim 2340b) https://sunnah.com/muslim:2340b

Hadith (Bukhari 5900) https://sunnah.com/bukhari:5900

Hadith (Bukhari 2534) https://sunnah.com/bukhari:2534

Hadith (Muslim 1438a) https://sunnah.com/muslim:1438a

Hadith (Bukhari 7186) https://sunnah.com/bukhari:7186

Hadith (Ibn Majah 2529) https://sunnah.com/ibnmajah:2529

Hadith (Nasa'i 4184) https://sunnah.com/nasai:4184

Hadith (Dawud 3358) https://sunnah.com/abudawud:3358

Hadith (Ibn Majah 2523) https://sunnah.com/ibnmajah:2523

Hadith (Tirmidhi 1239) https://sunnah.com/tirmidhi:1239

Hadith (Ibn Majah 2517) https://sunnah.com/ibnmajah:2517

Hadith (Dawud 1611) https://sunnah.com/abudawud:1611

Hadith (Muslim 1111e) https://sunnah.com/muslim:1111e

CHAPTER TEN

WHEN IS DECEPTION O.K.?

Getting an honest answer may depend on who you ask

D eception, utilized in the 'cause of Allah,' is a legally permitted strategy found in the primary Islamic doctrine and jurisprudence. There are several forms of deception, which can be used in many ways.

Recommended by Islamic law as a 'safe alternative' to 'lying' tawriya is when a speaker/writer asserts something that is technically true, but gives a misleading impression to the listener/reader. As such, the doctrine of tawriya permits deception in almost any situation provided that the lie is told in such a way that it is technically true.

- "Scholars say that there is no harm in giving a misleading impression if required by an interest countenanced by Sacred Law..." (1).

In 2023, Elmira Aghawaby, Canada's 'Special Representative on Combatting Islamophobia', noted on several occasions that hate crimes (the stats are actually termed hate and 'suspected' hate) against the Muslim community rose by 71% between 2020 and 2021 (2)(3).

She did not mention that in the same time period hate crimes against Catholics increased by 260% or that hate crimes against the Jewish community far exceeds any other (4). Neither did she mention that both the Koran and Hadith are decidedly antisemitic (5).

Utilizing that same data objectively, it is important to note that there were 487 hate crimes reported against a Jewish population of only 335,000. The Islamic population is 5.3 times larger, at 1.776 million. and reported 144 such crimes. This works out to one Muslim in 12,333 reporting a hate or 'suspected hate' crime, and 1 Jew in 688 (see chart below).

Number of police-reported hate crimes motivated by religion, Canada, 2018 to 2021, number				
	2018	2019	2020	2021
Jewish	372	306	331	487
Muslim	166	182	84	144
Catholic	44	51	43	155
Other[1]	52	57	40	64
Religion not specified	23	17	32	34

Jew hatred was therefore 18X higher per capita in than hate against the Islamic community - but Jews were given no Special Representative for 'phobias' against them, and neither were the Catholics.

In the year 2022-23 – hate crimes against Jews in Canada continued to increase and in fact doubled in that one year alone (6). Since October 2023, hate crimes against Jews have increased exponentially around the entire globe.

Why is that? And why has it taken so long for authorities to admit the steady rise in antisemitism in Canada? (7)

It is worth remembering that the multi-culturalism celebrated in 1970's Canada was inclusive. Everyone welcome to celebrate together at folk fests instead of a multitude of special days for special interest groups. Canada Day represented all the people of Canada, united.

For a few, division and deception may be politically expedient - but is a special day and representative for 'Islamophobia' justified and does it serve to unite or divide?

Sources:

(1) Sharia, 'Reliance of the Traveller' (r8.2, r10.2-3), Nuh Ha Mim Keller, Amana Publications 2015
https://archive.org/details/relianceofthetravellertheclassicmanualofislamicsacredlaw

(2) Speech to Senate Committee on Human Rights (3:57)
https://youtu.be/EOBqfOnSk4A

(3) Special Representative twitter:
https://twitter.com/AmiraElghawaby/status/1555328104738029568

(4) Chart: Statistics Canada 'Number of police-reported hate crimes motivated by religion, Canada, 2018 to 2021'
https://www150.statcan.gc.ca/n1/daily-quotidien/230322/cg-a004-eng.htm

(5) Doctrinal analysis:
https://www.cspii.org/learn-political-islam/methodology/statistical-analysis-political-islam/anti-jew-text-trilogy/

(6) CBC News:
https://www.cbc.ca/news/politics/bnai-brith-antisemitic-report-record-high-1.7195197

(7) Reuters:
https://www.reuters.com/world/trudeau-says-canada-faces-scary-rise-antisemitism-after-war-middle-east-2023-10-18/

EDUCATIONAL VIDEO: Deception
https://www.youtube.com/watch?v=9eP8tnQEWf8&t=2s

RELEVANT DOCTRINE:

Koran 2:225 https://legacy.quran.com/2/225

Koran 66:2 https://legacy.quran.com/66/2

Koran 5:89 https://legacy.quran.com/5/89

Koran 9:1 https://legacy.quran.com/9/1

Koran 48:29 https://legacy.quran.com/48/29

Koran 3:28 [Tafsir Ibn Kathir Sura 3, p.49]
https://archive.org/details/TafseerIbnKathirenglish114SurahsComplete/003Imran/

Hadith (Bukhari 2692) https://sunnah.com/bukhari:2692

Hadith (Bukhari 2947) https://sunnah.com/bukhari:2947

Hadith (Bukhari 3030) https://sunnah.com/bukhari:3030

Hadith (Nasa'i 3784) https://sunnah.com/nasai:3785

CHAPTER ELEVEN

IS MIGRANT INTEGRATION A PROBLEM IN THE EU?

During his recent speech in Marseilles, Pope Francis said there is no 'migrant emergency' and that migrants need to be 'integrated' (1)(2).

This is one point of view but is it reasonable to assume that everyone shares it? Looked at from the migrant's perspective, perhaps lack of integration has not been a failure at all.

Not all cultures share an enthusiasm for multiculturalism and – although it is rarely spoken of – a few are decidedly, and determinedly, monocultural.

This is not the 'fault' of the host country or its citizens who, if they are being true to the concept of 'multiculturalism' as it is currently being defined, should not be trying to integrate migrants that do not want to be integrated (3). Particularly if the migrants culture specifically forbids it.

So why are Europeans being chastised as 'nationalistic' and 'narrow minded' when it comes to welcoming and integrating new migrants? Such accusations stem from a lack of knowledge as to the foundational beliefs of the culture which is being introduced.

For example, in Islam integration can be very risky "... Whoever changed his Islamic religion, then kill him." (Bukhari 6922)

It is not uncommon for such a sentence to be enforced (4)(5).

Looked at in this light, an attitude of self-reproach on the part of the host country seems very curious (6). After all, is it the Pope who gets to determine whether or not lack of integration is a failure?

To answer this question the Islamic foundational doctrine can, and frequently does, speak very well for itself:

From the Koran:

- 5:51 O you who have believed, do not take the Jews and the Christians as allies. They are [in fact] allies of one another. And whoever is an ally to them among you - then indeed, he is [one] of them. Indeed, Allah guides not the wrongdoing people.

- 3:118 O you who have believed, do not take as intimates those other than yourselves, for they will not spare you [any] ruin. They wish you would have hardship. Hatred has already appeared from their mouths, and what their breasts conceal is greater. We have certainly made clear to you the signs, if you will use reason.

- 4:144 O you who have believed, do not take the disbelievers as allies instead of the believers. Do you wish to give Allah against yourselves a clear case?

From the Hadith:

- 'Abdullah said, "The best talk is Allah's Book (Qur'an), and the best guidance is the guidance of Muhammad." (Bukhari 6098)

There are many more such verses but these are enough to demonstrate that multiculturalism is not a value that is universally aspired to. This being the case, is it reasonable to expect that adherents to Islam will relinquish their sincere and deeply held belief in the words of Allah and Mohammed, whom they follow, to meet the expectations of those they have been explicitly instructed not to trust?

So whose yardstick should be used to measure success? Perhaps the dilemma lies in professing to be multi-cultural, but then using your own yardstick as a guide and being dismayed at the results (7).

Sources:

(1) France 24 video: 9:15, 14:15, 18:32
https://www.youtube.com/watch?v=gm-kQPK-VdU&t=1s

(2) News:
https://www.catholicnewsagency.com/news/249560/pope-francis-failure-to-integrate-migrants-can-create-serious-problems

(3) Multiculturalism def.:
https://www.britannica.com/topic/multiculturalism

(4) Uganda news:
https://www.christianpost.com/news/christian-convert-killed-in-uganda-for-leaving-islam.html

(5) Iraq news:
https://www.opendoors.org/en-US/research-reports/articles/stories/iraq-christian-convert-killed-by-family/

(6) Murray, Douglas 'The Strange Death of Europe, Immigration, Identity, Islam' Chap. 10 'The Tyranny of Guilt' p.157 Bloomsbury 2017

(7) Kassam, Raheem 'No Go Zones', Regnery Publishing 2017

RELEVANT DOCTRINE:

Koran 13:41 https://legacy.quran.com/13/41

Koran 4:144 https://legacy.quran.com/4/144

Koran 5:51 https://legacy.quran.com/5/51

Koran 3:118 https://legacy.quran.com/3/118

Hadith (Bukhari 6922) https://sunnah.com/bukhari:6922

Hadith (Bukhari 6098) https://sunnah.com/bukhari:6098

CHAPTER TWELVE

IS THERE FREEDOM OF RELIGION IN ISLAM?

Young TikTokers flaunting newly purchased Korans are trending these days so I purchased one to check the translation (1). Unsurprisingly, it was greatly simplified and in it Koran 4:34 now reads that it is permissible to 'spank' rather than 'beat' your wife (2).

While it is well known that to join Islam, it is only necessary to say the Shahada – 'there is no God but Allah and Mohammed is his messenger' (the 1st pillar of Islam and whispered into the ear of a newborn child) it is more important to know that leaving Islam is an entirely different matter.

Foundational Islamic doctrine, the 'ordained way of sharia' (Koran 45:18), makes it clear that to apostatize (which can also be accomplished by deliberately not attending to obligatory prayers) is punishable by death (3). Easy to join, not so easy to leave.

One such case that made headlines recently was that of a planned attack on a well known woman in England (4). The man who was arrested had converted *to Islam*, while she had converted *away from Islam*, and yet Islamic doctrine maintains that her decision, unlike his own, was deserving of death.

In addition to the demands of sharia, there are thirteen Islamic majority countries that impose capital punishment for apostasy from Islam or blasphemy (5).

An oft quoted sura (that there is freedom of religion) is Koran 109 'to you is your religion and to me is mine'. This verse dates back to the beginning of Mohammed's preaching long before his migration to Medina and the start of the Islamic calendar. The earlier verses of the Koran were intolerant but not violent and neither was there armed jihad. That changed after Mohammed's migration to Medina.

It is on the basis of Koran 2:106 that the later verses are considered better or stronger. This is the dualistic nature of Islamic doctrine – weak verses can be used at any time (depending on the situation and their usefulness) even though many have been superseded by later verses.

- "We do not abrogate a verse or cause it to be forgotten except that We bring forth [one] better than it or similar to it." A later verse is Koran 8:12 "...I will cast terror into the hearts of those who disbelieved, so strike [them] upon the necks and strike from them every fingertip."

Koran 4:89 specifically instructs believers to kill those who have turned away from Islam "...if they turn away, then seize them and kill them wherever you find them and take not from among them any ally or helper."

And Koran 4:80 states that "He who obeys the Messenger [Mohammed] has obeyed Allah..." There are numerous hadith where Mohammed states quite clearly that apostates should be killed:

- Dawud 4360 When a slave runs away and reverts to polytheism, he may lawfully be killed.

- Bukhari 7157 "He embraced Islam and then reverted back to Judaism." Mu'adh said, "I will not sit down unless you kill him (as it is) the verdict of Allah and His Apostle.

- Bukhari 6922 '...Whoever changed his Islamic religion, then kill him.'

According to Islamic doctrine, Muslim children have no freedom of choice in their religion. In the hadith Mohammed said that all children are born Muslim, it is their parent that corrupts them to become Christians, Jews or pagans. (Bukhari 1359)

After the death of Mohammed many people tried to leave Islam, resulting in the 'Ridda' (Apostasy) wars and thousands were slaughtered (6).

The Constitutions of non-Islamic countries and the Universal Declaration of Human Rights demand freedom of religion for their constituents (7). Other belief systems may not be so easy to join, but can be left without consequence and are therefore compatible with this requirement. Islam is not.

Something to think about.

Sources:

(1) Tiktokers:
https://www.youtube.com/watch?v=eOM_hoF8UxE&t=1s

(2) Tiktokers Koran
https://www.goodreads.com/book/show/54628184-the-qur-an

(3) Sharia, Reliance of the Traveller (w18:10) Nuh Ha Mim Keller, Amana Publications 2015
https://archive.org/details/relianceofthetravellertheclassicmanualofislamicsacredlaw

(4) UK News
https://www.theepochtimes.com/world/muslim-convert-jailed-for-life-for-plotting-to-kill-christian-preacher-at-speakers-corner-5547564?ea_src=ca-frontpage&ea_med=world-left-2

(5) Countries where apostasy is death:
https://www.indy100.com/news/the-countries-where-apostasy-is-punishable-by-death-7294486

(6) Apostasy and Ridda wars:
https://wikiislam.net/wiki/Islam_and_Apostasy

(7) Universal Declaration of Human Rights Article 18:
https://www.ohchr.org/sites/default/files/UDHR/Documents/UDHR_Translations/eng.pdf

EDUCATIONAL VIDEO: Tiktokers. Is there freedom of religion in Islam?
https://www.youtube.com/watch?v=hsaRsGw45Rk&t=9s

RELEVANT DOCTRINE:

Koran 2:106 https://legacy.quran.com/2/106

Koran 4:34 https://legacy.quran.com/4/34

Koran 4:80 https://legacy.quran.com/4/80

Koran 4:89 https://legacy.quran.com/4/89

Koran 4:103 https://legacy.quran.com/4/103

Koran 45:18 https://legacy.quran.com/45/18

Koran 109:1-6 https://legacy.quran.com/109

Koran 8:12 https://legacy.quran.com/8/12

Koran 8:17 https://legacy.quran.com/8/17

Hadith (Dawud 4360) https://sunnah.com/abudawud:4360

Hadith (Bukhari 7157) https://sunnah.com/bukhari:7157

Hadith (Bukhari 6922) https://sunnah.com/bukhari:6922

Hadith (Bukhari 1359) https://sunnah.com/bukhari:1359

Chapter Thirteen

How Does Sharia Define 'Good'?

And how do you...

What do you mean "if it's any good? – It makes money like crazy" he said, "of course it's good!"

The man was truly shocked by my question and I was shocked at his answer. I thought 'good' meant the consumer would get well. He thought 'good' meant the vendor would get rich! We both just gaped at each other in disbelief.

Two very different perspectives on what constitutes 'good'. Good for who?

And what about the one it's not so good for? The cheated consumer, or the disappointed constituent.

What do words really mean anyway? Unless we are using the same frame of reference, in reality, not much.

What immediately springs to mind is a verse from the Koran I was reading yesterday.

- Koran 2:216 "Fighting is prescribed for you, and ye dislike it. But it is possible that ye dislike a thing which is good for you, and that ye love a thing which is bad for you. But Allah knoweth, and ye know not.

It says fighting is 'good' for you. And you don't know but Allah does. Now this is the crux of the issue. Allah knows and humans do not – reason, need not apply.

So exactly what are practitioners of Islam allowed to figure out for themselves?

For example, at an on-line conference hosted by an Italian University I asked an 'expert' on the subject of Hijabs a question about Koran 33:59 – that a believing woman must cover herself so she will be 'known and not be assaulted'.

I asked if this did not then pose a risk for all unbelieving women as they would be the opposite – 'known' as available to be assaulted? Her answer – this is from a recognized expert – was to say that this was a 'theological question' that she 'could not answer.'

Why is she not able to answer?

From 'Reliance of the Traveller'(ROT) a handbook of sharia law (1):

- According to sharia the vast majority should "...refrain from discussing the subtleties of scholastic theology, lest corruption difficult to eliminate find its way into their basic religious convictions." (ROT a4.2)

- "...the good of the acts of those morally responsible is what the Lawgiver (syn Allah or His messenger) has indicated is good by permitting it or asking that it be done. And the bad is what the Lawgiver has indicated is bad by asking it not be done. The good is not what reason considers good, nor the bad what reason considers bad. The measures of good and bad... is the Sacred Law, not reason." (ROT a1.4)

- "By consensus of all scholars ...it is obligatory for the ordinary person to follow the scholar who is a mujtahid [expert in Islamic law]." (ROT b.7)

For Islam – Sharia defines what is 'good' and must not be questioned. This is Islam in practice – 'the ordained way' set out in the Koran and Hadith. When non-Islamic governments accommodate sharia they are supporting a system that is known globally for its many practices that run contrary to the Universal Declaration of Human Rights.

In this case 'good' is more than just a question of taste.

- "After Mecca, there is no hijra (migration) only jihad and good intentions." (Bukhari 2783)

Good for who or what?

Sharia?

Sources:

(1) Sharia, Reliance of the Traveller (a1.4, a4.2, b.7) Nuh Ha Mim Keller, Amana Publications 2015
https://archive.org/details/relianceofthetravellertheclassicmanualofislamicsacredlaw

RELEVANT DOCTRINE:

Koran 5:101-102 https://legacy.quran.com/5/101-102

Koran 45:18 https://legacy.quran.com/45/18

Koran 33:59 https://legacy.quran.com/33/59

Koran 16:43 https://legacy.quran.com/16/43

Koran 2:216 https://legacy.quran.com/2/216

Hadith (Bukhari 2783) https://sunnah.com/bukhari/56/2

CHAPTER FOURTEEN

WHAT IS SHARIA?

And why everyone needs to know...

S haria law is the 'ordained way' of Islam, (Koran 45:18) the teachings found in the Koran and Hadith of Mohammed that believers are expected to adhere to. Some are obligatory, others are recommended, permitted, discouraged or forbidden (1). If Mohammed commanded something then it's obligatory, if he forbid something, then it is 'haram'. If it's something he did but didn't command then it's recommended etc.

Sharia is currently being implemented across non-Islamic societies and we can expect a few, such as the United Kingdom, (with over 85 sharia courts where a woman's testimony is worth half a man's) to be fully under the control of sharia very soon (2). They may not know exactly how that happened but knowledgeable observers certainly do.

This transformation of non-Islamic countries is accomplished through the accommodation of sharia (Islamic) finance, government regulation (i.e. blasphemy laws aka 'Islamophobia'), conflicted advisors, uninformed human rights tribunals, trade & business, a never ending barrage of activist organization lobbying, letter writing campaigns, actions and events affecting schools, museums, the justice system, hospitals, recreation centres, restaurants and even cartoons. The largest Sharia 'halal' expo in North America is held in Canada every year promoting sharia compliant finance, insurance, vacations and every kind of product imaginable (3).

For this reason, it should be no surprise that now in 2024, young TikTokers are converting to Islam to show their support for Gaza – a situation that has evolved over the course of an entire century and which – like sharia – the majority of them know next to nothing about. On-line and other influencers play a significant role.

By overlooking the fact that sharia does not recognize equality before the law or freedom of religion, most non-Islamic countries are not exercising the necessary precautions to resist the incursion of sharia through Islamic organizational infrastructure (4). They simply lack the knowledge to do so. When advice is needed, rather than taking a non-Islamic view they call on Islamic leaders for advice which frequently results in the introduction of even more accommodation to sharia under the guise of multiculturalism. (Koran 45:18)

With no diversion from the current trajectory, continual demands on non-Islamic countries (i.e. 61 NCCM Recommendations) (5) together with a lack of knowledge as to the nature of sharia (6), naïve virtue signalling, and demographic growth make it inevitable that non-Islamic countries will all be living under sharia soon. There is a critical tipping point at which the process cannot be reversed.

Sources:

(1) Manual of Sharia law: 'Reliance of the Traveller,' (Book C 'Types of Human Acts' c2.1-c2.5) Nuh Ha Mim Keller, Amana Pub. 2015 https://archive.org/details/relianceofthetravellertheclassicmanualofislamicsacredlaw

(2) Sharia, the Cairo Declaration and the European Convention of Human Rights (Resolution 2253 2019)

https://assembly.coe.int/nw/xml/XRef/Xref-XML2HTML-en.asp?fileid=253
53

(3) Halal Expo:
https://halalexpocanada.com/index.html

(4) Foreign funding of 'radical' mosques:
https://www.europarl.europa.eu/doceo/document/E-9-2022-000345_EN.htm
l

(5) Canada Summit 'Islamophobia'
https://www.nccm.ca/wp-content/uploads/2021/06/Policy-Recommendation
s_NCCM.pdf

(6) Manual of Sharia law: 'Reliance of the Traveller', Nuh Ha Mim Keller, Amana
Pub. 2015
https://archive.org/details/relianceofthetravellertheclassicmanualofislamicsacre
dlaw

CHAPTER FIFTEEN

POLYGAMY AND THE IMPLEMENTATION OF SHARIA LAW IN NON-ISLAMIC COUNTRIES

H ow many wives are permitted in say – Germany?

According to sharia – four. You may think this only happens in Islamic countries but that would be wrong. For example, in Germany, there is no requirement for Imams to register marriages. To marry a second, third or fourth wife without acknowledging the first, it is only necessary to use a different Imam. The situation is problematic for social services because many women, who appear to be married, are collecting benefits and experiencing difficulties, but higher levels of government seem unwilling to acknowledge or address it (1)(2)(3).

- "...marry other women of your choice, two, or three, or four" (Koran 4:3)

It is in this manner that through the practice of sharia – the ordained way of Islam - parallel legal systems are being introduced and contribute to the Islamisation of non-Islamic countries.

In the UK, there are over 85 sharia courts where a woman's testimony is worth half that of a man's (4). In 2019, the EU Parliamentary Assembly reported that:

- "members of the Muslim community, sometimes voluntarily, often under considerable social pressure, accept their religious jurisdiction mainly in marital issues and Islamic divorce proceedings but also in matters relating to inheritance and Islamic commercial contracts. The Assembly is concerned that the rulings of the Sharia councils clearly discriminate against women in divorce and inheritance cases. The Assembly is aware that informal Islamic courts may also exist in other Council of Europe member States" (5).

Mohammed's wife Aisha said, "I have not seen any woman suffering as much as the believing women. Look! Her skin is greener than her clothes!" Books can be purchased describing how to beat wives properly (6) and they suffer in the next world as well – Mohammed said:

- "O women! Give alms, as I have seen that the majority of the dwellers of Hell-fire were you (women)." They asked, "Why is it so, O Allah's Messenger?" He replied, "You curse frequently and are ungrateful to your husbands. I have not seen anyone more deficient in intelligence and religion than you..." (Bukhari 304)

Whether in Canada or elsewhere, multiple marriages can occur wherever Islam is practiced as this is the husband's right according to sharia (7).

- Mohammed said "... If I were to command anyone to make prostration before another I would command women to prostrate themselves before their husbands, because of the special right over them given to husbands by Allah." (Dawud 2140)

Keep in mind that a Muslim man can divorce his wife any time he wants to by simply saying 'I divorce you'. The third time he does this he cannot take her back without her marrying someone else first. Women with children are thereby placed in an untenable situation and may resort to a 'temporary marriage' so she can return to them (8)(9). Conversely, a woman needs her husband's permission to divorce (10).

According to a handbook of sharia "The husband is only obliged to support his wife when she gives herself to him or offers to, meaning she allows him full enjoyment of her person and does not refuse him sex at any time of the night or day " (11).

Mohammed had 13 wives (12) and there was no limit to the number of sex slaves 'that the right hand possesses' for himself or his followers. Child marriage is permitted for the same reason, Mohammed married Aisha when she was six and consummated the marriage when she was nine.

Koran 65:4 The Divorce' specifies the waiting period for "... those who have not menstruated..." is three months. In Iran, over 7,000 girls under the age of 14 were married in only 3 months in 2020 (13) and a virgin child may be married without her consent (14).

- "Your wives are a tilth for you, so go into your tilth when you like...' (Koran 2:223)

How many wives is the question.

Sources:

(1) German Documentary:
https://www.bitchute.com/video/Wn964C49ZNcu/

(2) Britain:
http://www.gees.org/articulos/britain-muslim-polygamists-to-get-more-we
lfare-benefits

(3) Canada op-ed:
https://ottawacitizen.com/opinion/polygamy-in-islam

(4) UK Sharia courts:

https://researchbriefings.files.parliament.uk/documents/CDP-2019-0102/CDP-2019-0102.pdf

(5) EU Parliamentary Assembly #8:

https://assembly.coe.int/nw/xml/XRef/Xref-XML2HTML-en.asp?fileid=25353

(6) Canada:

https://web.archive.org/web/20170202090249/https://torontosun.com/2012/03/23/book-tells-muslim-men-how-to-beat-and-control-their-wives

(7) Canada:

https://www.cbc.ca/news/canada/polygamy-canadian-muslim-community-1.4971971

(8) India:

https://indianexpress.com/article/india/kaun-shabana-noorpur-talaq-nikaah-halala-uttar-pradesh-5014479/

(9) BBC video: 'Halala – the Men Who Sell Divorce'
https://www.youtube.com/watch?v=TlvNMlIMWhw

(10) Sharia, Reliance of the Traveller (n1.0-1) Nuh Ha Mim Keller, Amana Publications 2015
https://archive.org/details/relianceofthetravellertheclassicmanualofislamicsacredlaw

(11) Ibid (m11.9)

(12) Guillaume, Alfred. 'The Life of Muhammad: a Translation of Ishaq's Sirat Rasul Allah' p.792 Oxford University Press, 1967
https://archive.org/details/history-ibn-ishaq-sirat-rasul-allah-the-life-of-muhammad/page/n7/mode/2up

(13) Iran:
https://women.ncr-iran.org/2020/12/02/child-marriages-in-iran-over-7000-girl
s-under-14-got-married-in-3-months/

(14) Sharia, Reliance of the Traveller (m3.13) Nuh Ha Mim Keller, Amana
Publications 2015
https://archive.org/details/relianceofthetravellertheclassicmanualofislamicsacre
dlaw

India – Muslim Personal Law Board (sharia):
https://en.wikipedia.org/wiki/All_India_Muslim_Personal_Law_Board

India:
https://organiser.org/2023/05/27/175896/bharat/uttarakhand-high-court-issu
es-notice-to-muslim-personal-law-board-in-case-seeking-ban-on-marriage-of-mi
nor-girls/

Journal:
https://journals.sagepub.com/doi/full/10.1177/2321023019838648

EDUCATIONAL VIDEO:
Did Islam improve the lives of women?
https://www.youtube.com/watch?v=NZPViZj3kvw

RELEVANT DOCTRINE:

Koran 4:3 https://legacy.quran.com/4/3

Koran 4:34 https://legacy.quran.com/4/34

Koran 65:4 https://legacy.quran.com/65/4

Koran 24:31 https://legacy.quran.com/24/31

Hadith (Bukhari 5825) https://sunnah.com/bukhari:5825

Hadith (Bukhari 3894) https://sunnah.com/bukhari:3894

Hadith (Bukhari 304) https://sunnah.com/bukhari:304

Hadith (Dawud 2146) https://sunnah.com/abudawud:2146

Hadith (Dawud 2140) https://sunnah.com/abudawud:2140

Hadith (Ibn Majah 1986) https://sunnah.com/ibnmajah:1986

CHAPTER SIXTEEN

DO YOU KNOW WHO A TERRORIST IS?

Most people think they do — well, maybe it's time to think again

In 2022, a young mother from the U.K. holidaying in Saudi Arabia was sentenced to 34 years in jail for her tweets. The original sentence had been 6 yrs. but increased by another 28 yrs. when she appealed (1). In September 2023, an 17 year old girl was sentenced to 18 years in jail for tweeting in support of political prisoners (2). This followed quick on the heels of the death sentence for a religious scholar, "They don't say he has created any kind of terrorist organisation. They literally say he has betrayed his religion and the state by following YouTube and Twitter accounts" (3). Such sentences are not uncommon.

The counter-terrorist law in Saudi Arabia criminalizes "calling for atheist thought in any form or calling into question the fundamentals of the Islamic religion" (4). And is so broad it can be taken to mean almost anything (5). Exactly who are such counter-terrorist laws intended to protect?

In Afghanistan, women are shrouded in black while holding flags which read "We are satisfied with the Islamic attitude and behavior of the mujaheddin" (6). Are they terrorists if they don't support the jihadis, and do they have any choice? It's a good question.

The definition of terrorism then clearly depends very much on who is saying it and where it is being said. When participants holding widely diverging definitions of terrorism meet to discuss 'global counter-terrorism' (7) – how is accurate communication possible?

Correct and explicit terminology were never more important. Plain speaking rather than 'political correctness'.

Islamic foundational doctrine states that to be martyred as a jihadi will be rewarded with paradise, and that jihad is the best deed.(al-Nasa'i 2624) In the Bukhari Hadith (stories and traditions of Mohammed) 98% of jihad is violent, although it can and does take other forms (8)(9).

Given the foregoing, donations to an Islamic organization to fight terrorism cannot be expected to combat jihadis. They can be expected to fight who, and where? How will donations be used in the host country? And if the funds are shared overseas, could they be used to help put a 17 year old girl in jail for 18 years?

And finally, how did Sweden come to be referred to as 'the jihadist hub of Scandinavia' and did the use of euphemisms instead of concrete terms play a role in this? (10)

Objective naming is crucial, using accurate and precise words which clearly and unambiguously identify who and what we are speaking of. Terrorist, is not one of them. Jihad is, but the term is rarely heard even though such attacks are occurring around the globe on an almost daily basis (11).

The numerous battles of Mohammed and the doctrinal imperative (12) to emulate him are similarly given scant attention save that of his followers (13). By disregarding the significance of Mohammed – the doctrine and his example, non-Islamic participants lack essential information in any discussion concerning jihad.

- Mohammed said, "The person who participates in (Holy battles) in Allah's cause and nothing compels him to do so except belief in Allah and His Apostles, will be recompensed by Allah either with a reward, or booty (if he survives) or will be admitted to Paradise (if he is killed in the battle as a martyr). Had I not found it difficult for my followers, then I would not remain behind any sariya* going for Jihad and I would have loved to be martyred in Allah's cause and then made alive, and then martyred and then made alive, and then again martyred in His cause.'" (Bukhari 36)

* A 'sariya' is a military expedition that Mohammed did not personally participate in, a 'ghazwah' is what they were called when he did personally take part. Mohammed was involved in a battle on average of one every 6.5 weeks for the last nine years of his life (14).

Sources:

(1) Saudi Arabia:
https://www.middleeasteye.net/news/saudi-arabia-women-rights-defender-prison-tweets

(2) Saudi Arabia:
https://www.zerohedge.com/geopolitical/saudi-arabia-sentences-schoolgirl-18-years-prison-over-tweets

(3) Saudi Arabia:
https://www.middleeasteye.net/news/saudi-arabia-saeed-ghamdi-brother-scholar-sentenced-death-tweets

(4) Library of Congress:
https://www.loc.gov/item/global-legal-monitor/2014-02-04/saudi-arabia
-new-terrorism-law-in-effect/

(5) U.S. State Dept.
https://www.state.gov/reports/2021-report-on-international-religious-free
dom/saudi-arabia/

(6) Afghanistan:
https://orf.at/stories/3228222/

(7) Saudi Arabia:
https://english.alarabiya.net/News/2013/02/16/Global-counter-terrorism
-conference-opens-in-Saudi-Arabia

(8) Statistical Analysis:
https://www.cspii.org/learn-political-islam/methodology/statistical-analysi
s-extra-information/lesser-jihad/

(9) MCDC Project:
https://assets.publishing.service.gov.uk/media/5a8228a540f0b62305b92ca
a/dar_mcdc_hybrid_warfare.pdf

(10) BBC How Sweden Became an Exporter of Jihad
https://www.bbc.com/news/magazine-37578919

(11) Jihad reports:
https://thereligionofpeace.com

(12) Doctrinal imperative:
https://cspi-web-media.ams3.cdn.digitaloceanspaces.com/documents/The
_Sunna_of_Mohammed.pdf

(13) Memri TV:

https://www.memri.org/tv/released-hamas-terrorist-ahlam-tamimi-glorifies-ma
rtyrdom-jihad-operations

(14) Guillaume, Alfred. 'The Life of Muhammad: a Translation of Ishaq's Sirat
Rasul Allah' (p. 659-660). Oxford University Press, 1967
https://archive.org/details/GuillaumeATheLifeOfMuhammad/page/n3/mode/
2up

RELEVANT DOCTRINE:

Koran 9:111 https://legacy.quran.com/9/111

Koran 61:11 https://legacy.quran.com/61/11

Koran 9:73 https://legacy.quran.com/9/73

Hadith (Bukhari 36) https://sunnah.com/bukhari:36

Hadith (Bukhari 4046) https://sunnah.com/bukhari:4046

Hadith (Bukhari 6098) https://sunnah.com/bukhari:6098

Hadith (Bukhari 3030) https://sunnah.com/bukhari:3030

CHAPTER SEVENTEEN

GEOPOLITICAL AND FINANCIAL INFLUENCE OF ISLAM

Sharia abounds in non-Islamic countries

The stated goal of Islam is world domination.(Ibn Majah 3952) The seeds to achieve this are political and lie in the foundational doctrine itself, whether or not it is the personal goal of an individual (1).

To deny that Allah's religion is to be followed by the entire world is apostasy and the 'ugliest form of unbelief' – kufr' (2) Mohammed said "I have been commanded to fight against people till they testify that there is no god but Allah, that Muhammad is the messenger of Allah..." (Muslim 22)

Islamic doctrine is found in the Koran and Hadith and describes the 'ordained way' Muslims are supposed to adhere to – this is Sharia (Koran 45:18).

Because instructions pertaining to almost every facet of life are described in the Koran and Hadith, and because Muslims are obliged to conform to this if possible – every demand for Sharia that is conceded to by non-Islamic countries means that Muslims must now utilize it if they can.

Even though a 2004 UK Study (3) found that '75% of Muslims were indifferent to shari'a finance', once there is a Sharia alternative, Muslims who may have been perfectly happy with their conventional mortgage, nail polish, or brand of peanut butter will now be pressured by entities within the 'ummah' – the global community of Islam - to select the Islamic option (4).

Believing this to be a 'good thing' many non-Muslims will also happily participate, eating halal food, donating to Islamic charities or investing in 'Islamic ethical finance', which are Sharia compliant, and thereby aid in the expansion of Sharia (5)(6).

In addition to this, the halal industry contributes to an Islamic tax of 2.5% called 'zakat' - often referred to as an Islamic 'charity'. The seventh category of zakat is to finance jihad, which Sharia describes as a 'communal obligation'. (Koran 9:60)

What about Darura?

There is another way – 'Darura' – 'necessity overcomes obligation' or 'necessity makes the forbidden permissible' (7)(8)(9). Darura is frequently practiced in non-Islamic countries and is consistent with Islamic doctrine. (Koran 16:115)

If halal fingernail polish, Islamic swim schedules at the rec centre, Sharia approved insurance, or mortgages are not available – then darura applies and a Muslim is free to choose the non-Sharia alternative.

Perhaps acceding to ongoing demands for Sharia compliance of all kinds, is not being kind to Muslims, or to non-Muslims after all?

- Mohammed said "Indeed Allah gathered the earth for me so that I saw its east and its west. And surely my Ummah's authority shall reach over all that was shown to me of it..." (Muslim 2889a)

Sources:

(1) Ibrahim, Abraham, Gatestone Institute Aug 14, 2023
https://www.gatestoneinstitute.org/19884/jihad-in-austria

(2) Sharia, Reliance of the Traveller (Apostasy) o8.0, o8.7, o8.7 (7, 20), o9.1,
o9.4, w.4.3, Nuh Ha Mim Keller, Amana Publications 2015
https://archive.org/details/relianceofthetravellertheclassicmanualofislamics
acredlaw

(3) Sookhdeo, Dr. Patrick 'Understanding Shari'a Finance' Isaac Publishing,
2008 p.78-79

(4) Fatah, Tarek, Toronto Sun June 22, 2019
https://torontosun.com/opinion/columnists/fatah-shariah-law-makes-a-co
meback-in-ontario

(5) 'Shari'ah Standards' The Accounting and Auditing Organization for
Islamic Finance 2017, Section 35 (9) p 896
https://aaoifi.com/shariaa-standards/?lang=en

(6) Canadian Halal Investments:
https://woodgundyadvisors.cibc.com/web/khaled-sultan/halal-investing?la
ng=en_US

(7) Brill Encyclopedia (darura):
https://referenceworks.brillonline.com/entries/encyclopaedia-of-islam-2/da
rura-SIM_1730

(8) University of Exeter (darura):
https://ore.exeter.ac.uk/repository/handle/10036/112862

(9) Oxford Reference (darura):
https://www.oxfordreference.com/display/10.1093/oi/authority.20110810
104722491

VIDEO: Darura to perform jihad 1:15 https://www.bitchute.com/video/8S9 4Y9E7z8Fy/

RELEVANT DOCTRINE:

Koran 45:18 https://legacy.quran.com/45/18

Koran 16:115 https://legacy.quran.com/16/115

Koran 39:53 https://legacy.quran.com/39/53

Hadith (Bukhari 3167) https://sunnah.com/bukhari:3167

Hadith (Tirmidhi 2176) https://sunnah.com/tirmidhi:2176

Hadith (Ibn Majah 3952) https://sunnah.com/ibnmajah:3952

Hadith (Bukhari 3167) https://sunnah.com/bukhari:3167

Hadith (Muslim 22) https://sunnah.com/muslim:22

Hadith (Muslim 2889a) https://sunnah.com/muslim:2889a

Hadith (Buhari 335) https://sunnah.com/bukhari:335

VIDEO: Darura to perform jihad 1:15 https://www.bitchute.com/video/8S9 4Y9E7z8Fy/

CHAPTER EIGHTEEN

CHARITY AND JIHAD

...Connecting the dots...

In 2010, a Canadian Islamic charity's status was revoked for providing over $14.6 million in support of Hamas or other terrorist entities. The charity was later listed as a terrorist entity under the criminal code (1)(2).

In 2011, a Canada Revenue Agency (CRA) audit of the Islamic Society of North America (ISNA) determined that only one dollar in four reached the poor and needy (3). In 2018, ISNA was suspended and fined $550,000 over concerns that they may have 'provided resources' to armed militants in Kashmir (4). Yet four years later the Canadian government gave ISNA $687,000 to build an Islamic Centre in Yellowknife NWT (5).

Currently, the ongoing investigation of an Islamic Charity by the CRA includes numerous allegations of supporting the Muslim Brotherhood and its connection to the designated jihadi terrorist organization Hamas, along with various breaches of tax law (6).

In return, the Canadian Revenue Agency is accused of Islamophobia (7).

It is the consistent reference to Jihad that is of interest here. Why is it that this same issue comes up repeatedly with Islamic charities? (8)

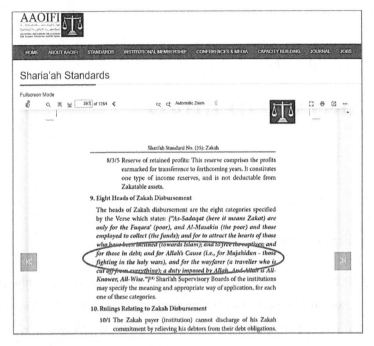

Canada is not alone in this.

The list of designated terrorist entities in non-Islamic countries invariably shows a preponderance of Islamic ones, all of whom require financing (9).

In Germany "associations and non-profit organizations enjoy a certain degree of protection, and investigations by authorities such as the Office for the Protection of the Constitution are limited when it comes to finances" (10). And in the U.K., a registered charity affiliated with terror links in Pakistan runs over 40 mosques as well as Islamic schools (11).

Charity/ Jihad – what is the connection?

Zakat is an obligatory Islamic tax of 2.5% often referred to as charity. It is one of the five pillars of Islam, and consequently produces an enormous amount of money to be used in accordance with the Koran and Hadith.

Non-Muslims also donate to Islamic charities.

Koran 9:60 (Khan)

- "As-Sadaqat (here it means Zakat) are only for the Fuqara' (poor), and Al-Masakin (the poor) and those employed to collect (the funds); and to attract the hearts of those who have been inclined (towards Islam); and to free the captives; and for those in debt; and for Allah's Cause (i.e. for Mujahidun – those fighting in the holy wars), and for the wayfarer (a traveller who is cut off from everything); a duty imposed by Allah. And Allah is All-Knower, All-Wise."

Hadith (Tirmidhi 2863)

- ... Mohammed said: "And I command you with five that Allah commanded me: Listening and obeying, Jihad, Hijrah [migration], and the Jama'ah....[congregational prayer]"

From 'Reliance of the Traveller, a Classic Manual of Islamic Sacred Law' (ROT)(12)

- "The seventh category is those fighting for Allah, meaning people engaged in Islamic military operations for whom no salary has been allotted in the army roster (0: but who are volunteers for jihad without remuneration)." (ROT h8.17)

- Jihad itself, is described as a communal obligation. (ROT o9.1)

It should be noted that Islamic charities that have been authorized to collect zakat can do so under various categories and in Canada, that authorization comes from the Canadian Council of Imams. At least one Canadian charity is specifically authorized to collect zakat under the category of 'fi Sabillillah' – the cause of Allah (13).

Many such Islamic organizations are registered as 'charities', this means that those who donate to them can obtain a receipt to use as a tax deduction thereby providing an additional financial incentive.

Islam is not the only religion to obligate a form of charity, but it is the only one in which financing jihad is not only legitimate, as per Sharia accounting standards, but also sanctified in the foundational doctrine (14).

- Koran 9:103 Take, [O, Muhammad], from their wealth a charity by which you purify them and cause them increase, and invoke [Allah 's blessings] upon them. Indeed, your invocations are reassurance for them. And Allah is Hearing and Knowing.

Sources:

(1) Letter of Intention to Revoke:
https://www.canadiancharitylaw.ca/uploads/01_20110309_NITR_with_
App_A,_B_and_C.pdf

(2) News Release: IRFAN Canada Terrorist Entity
https://web.archive.org/web/20140429154531/http://news.gc.ca/web/arti
cle-en.do?nid=843809

(3) Canada News:
https://www.thestar.com/news/gta/muslim-charity-squandered-money-for
-poor/article_9c64655f-ebb2-5dc5-aa9b-a7015d4acf1c.html

(4) Canada News:
https://globalnews.ca/news/4490892/cra-suspends-fines-major-islamic-cha
rity-over-concerns-it-may-have-provided-resources-to-armed-militants/

(5) Yellowknife, Canada News:
https://www.cbc.ca/news/canada/north/yellowknife-islamic-centre-constructio
n-summer-2023-1.6635657

(6) Canada News:
https://nationalpost.com/opinion/jamie-sarkonak-the-cras-complex-allegations
-of-systemic-islamophobia

(7) Canada News:
https://www.cbc.ca/news/politics/cra-nsira-muslim-charities-1.6778878

(8) Canadian Senate Hearings:
https://sencanada.ca/Content/Sen/Committee/441/RIDR/briefs/Follow-up
-CRAResponse_e.pdf

(9) Canada jihadi terrorists listed:
https://www.publicsafety.gc.ca/cnt/ntnl-scrt/cntr-trrrsm/lstd-ntts/crrnt-lstd-nt
ts-en.aspx

(10) Germany News:
https://www.dw.com/en/germany-takes-action-against-hamas-supporters/a-67
085873

(11) UK News:
https://www.meforum.org/64792/government-suspends-grant-to-uk-mosque
-after-fwi

(12) Sharia: Reliance of the Traveller (h8.17, o9.1) Nuh Ha Mim Keller, Amana
Publications 2015
https://archive.org/details/relianceofthetravellertheclassicmanualofislamicsacre
dlaw

(13) Canadian Charity Authorized to collect Zakat in 'cause of Allah' category:
https://www.nccm.ca/wp-content/uploads/2015/06/Letter_NCCM_Zakat_2
015.pdf

(14) Exclusivity of Islamic Charity:
https://www.thereligionofpeace.com/pages/quran/charity-disaster-relief.aspx

Image: Shari'ah Standards' The Accounting and Auditing Organization for Islamic Finance 2017, Section 35 (9) p 896
https://aaoifi.com/shariaa-standards/?lang=en

RELEVANT DOCTRINE:

Koran 2: 173 https://legacy.quran.com/2/173

Koran 5:3 https://legacy.quran.com/5/3

Koran 5:5 https://legacy.quran.com/5/5

Koran 9:60 https://legacy.quran.com/9/60

Koran 9:103 https://legacy.quran.com/9/103

Hadith (Bukhari 3666) https://sunnah.com/bukhari:3666

Hadith (Muslim 1027a) https://sunnah.com/muslim:1027a

Hadith (Ibn Majah 2397) https://sunnah.com/ibnmajah:2397

Hadith (Tirmidhi 2863) https://sunnah.com/tirmidhi:2863

Hadith (Nasa'i 3187) https://sunnah.com/nasai:3187

Hadith (Dawud 3025) https://sunnah.com/abudawud:3025

Chapter Nineteen

October 7th. Israel

The day ideology trumped humanity

Today, I am writing about women and in particular those women who were tortured, raped and killed in Israel on Oct 7th, 2023 at the hands of jihadis (1).

Non-Islamic countries are not accustomed to such barbarism against women and a shameful number of women's groups around the globe were either shocked into silence, or denied the facts even in the face of testimony and physical evidence that was shared with journalists, politicians and many others (2).

A dear friend of mine and veteran of Afghanistan could not eat or sleep for two days after viewing the official Israeli footage.

For those who are still incredulous it is important to understand that prolific antisemitism, low status of women, treatment of 'unbelievers' and of those captured and killed or enslaved as booty in foundational Islamic texts coalesced here and was visited upon innocent civilians in depraved ways too sadistic to describe (3).

Even today, torture, by means of cutting off limbs, crucifixion and stoning is carried out in Islamic countries (4). Sharia is enshrined not only in those states but also in the Cairo Declaration they subscribe to as members of the Organization of Islamic Cooperation (OIC) even though they are also members of the United

Nations (5). A U.N. that failed to condemn the rape and murder of these women for almost two months (6).

In the following months, over the drum of protesters in the streets and at Universities, the Islamic hadith 'the trees will say there is a Jew behind me, come and kill him' has been chanted by ill-informed mobs. Do they realize that:

- Koran 7:179 asserts that unbelievers are worse than cattle;

- Koran 33:50 captive women can be used as sex slaves; and

- Koran 8:12 asserts "...I will cast terror into the hearts of those who have disbelieved, so strike them over the necks, and smite all over all their fingers and toes.'

Most likely, they would say 'it's irrelevant', 'ancient history', nothing to do with Gaza. But just because Islamic doctrine means nothing to ill-informed mobs, it is pure projection to assume that the doctrine means nothing to those who sincerely believe in and follow it.

For believers and unbelievers alike, Islamic doctrine states that women lack intelligence and that most inhabitants of hell are women.(Bukhari 304) In many parts of the world women are still captured and used as sex slaves, ransomed or kept as booty, forced to convert and married against their will (7).

- Koran 33:59 requires 'believing' women to veil themselves so they will not be assaulted.

Unbelievers, who do not cover themselves are thus easily identified and become susceptible to attack, this is only lately being recognized internationally as an ongoing threat to women in non-Islamic states (8).

From a handbook of Sharia:

- "...the good of the acts of those morally responsible is what the Lawgiver

(Allah or His messenger) has indicated is good by permitting it or asking it be done. And the bad is what the Lawgiver has indicated is bad by asking it not be done..." (9)

In the course of my research I recall the account of an atrocity against an elderly woman, ordered by one of Mohammed's generals, that was so terrible I have never been able to forget it. (10)(11) The brutality perpetrated by jihadis, in the name of Allah, against the Jewish women of Israel on Oct 7th are in this same category but on a massive scale. Too horrific to describe in a public post but found in the references below.

Was Mohammed's general soundly punished? No, he was sent on more expeditions.

I want to honor that woman's memory today – her name was Umm Qirfa – along with the lives of all those young girls and women who suffered, and were slaughtered, at the hands of jihadis on October 7th. May they rest in peace.

Sources:

(1) Testimony of first responders to U.N.(22m – 31m)
https://www.youtube.com/watch?v=OXEu7lGOAl0

(2) World News:
https://www.theguardian.com/world/2023/dec/05/un-hears-accounts-of-sexual-violence-during-7-october-attacks-by-hamas

(3) Reliance of the Traveller (o10.2) Umdat al-Salik trans by Nuh Ha Mim Keller, Amana Publications 2015
https://archive.org/details/relianceofthetravellertheclassicmanualofislamicsacredlaw

(4) News Saudi Arabia
https://www.the-sun.com/news/3810902/saudi-arabia-executions-eye-gouging
-crucifixion/

(5) U.N. human rights conflict:
https://perspectivesonislam.substack.com/p/what-happens-when-declarations
-of

(6) U.N. 12/1/23
https://www.unwomen.org/en/news-stories/statement/2023/12/un-women-st
atement-on-the-situation-in-israel-and-gaza

(7) Iran News:
https://web.archive.org/web/20220519014026/https:/www.israelnationalnews
.com/news/133214

(8) News Austria
https://theliberal.ie/austrian-mp-claims-women-in-vienna-are-wearing-veils-to
-avoid-sexual-harassment-from-muslim-men/

(9) Reliance of the Traveller (a1.4, o10.2) Umdat al-Salik trans by Nuh Ha Mim
Keller, Amana Publications 2015
https://archive.org/details/relianceofthetravellertheclassicmanualofislamicsacre
dlaw

(10) Guillaume, Alfred. 'The Life of Muhammad: a Translation of Ishaq's Sirat
Rasul Allah', #980 p 664-665 (Umm Qirfa) Oxford University Press, 1967 (Ibn
Ishaq 700-767CE)
https://archive.org/details/history-ibn-ishaq-sirat-rasul-allah-the-life-of-muham
mad/page/n7/mode/2up

(11) The History of Al-Tabari: the Victory of Islam, trans. Michael Fishbein, vol.
8, SUNYP, 1997, pp. 95-97

RELEVANT DOCTRINE:

Koran 7:179 https://legacy.quran.com/7/179

Koran 8:12 https://legacy.quran.com/8/12

Koran 9:29 https://legacy.quran.com/9/29

Koran 33:50 https://legacy.quran.com/33/50

Koran 33:59 https://legacy.quran.com/33/59

Koran 5:51 https://legacy.quran.com/3/54

Koran 13:41 https://legacy.quran.com/13/41

Koran 3:54 https://legacy.quran.com/3/54

Koran 23:5-6 https://legacy.quran.com/23/5-6

Koran 68:2-4 https://legacy.quran.com/68/2-4

Hadith (Bukhari 2926) https://sunnah.com/bukhari:2926

Hadith (Bukhari 3167) https://sunnah.com/bukhari:3167

Hadith (Bukhari 3029) https://sunnah.com/bukhari:3029

Hadith (Bukhari 2229) https://sunnah.com/bukhari:2229

Hadith (Bukhari 304) https://sunnah.com/bukhari:304

Hadith (Dawud 2140) https://sunnah.com/abudawud:2140

Hadith (Muslim 2405) https://sunnah.com/muslim:2405

Hadith (Bukhari 2338) https://sunnah.com/bukhari:2338

Hadith (Bukhari 3122) https://sunnah.com/bukhari:3122

Bukhari (Muslim 2793) https://sunnah.com/muslim:2793

CHAPTER TWENTY

WHAT IS WAQF?

H amas is claiming Palestine is an Islamic Waqf so it is important to understand what that actually means.

In contrast to the common law of non-Islamic countries, an Islamic 'Waqf' is any property or real estate eternally dedicated 'in the name of Allah' through a 'restricted' endowment. Waqf property uses vary and may include such things as 'accumulating funds for Allah's cause', constructing a cemetery or building a mosque (1). It is the act of gifting, not the property itself, that is pious and brings eternal reward.

Once a property is transferred into Waqf, ownership rights terminate. Neither a giver, nor the state can ever change the Waqf status which is irrevocable, inalienable and expected to continue in perpetuity. While the basis for Waqf is found in Islamic doctrine, today it is usually regulated by a Waqf board and may be subject to Sharia accounting standards (2).

In India last year, an entire village discovered that the Waqf board claimed ownership of all – including their temple (3)(4).

Which brings us to Israel, the Hamas charter (below) and its reference to Waqf.

While the area of Palestine was part of the Ottoman Empire, it was never a recognized country with borders. And although the list of Ottoman conquests is lengthy, at times including most of Greece, Hungary, Armenia, Egypt and Iraq, it did fall just as other empires have fallen (5).

Many of these areas are still under Islamic authority, but not all - such as Israel, where every resident, regardless of race or creed, was immediately granted Israeli citizenship with full rights and privileges when the country was created (6)(7). It has been the target of Islamic jihad ever since.

It is worth remembering that at one time Spain was also under Islamic rule and that with Islamic authority comes Sharia. This does not always work out so well for non-Islamic residents, such as the recent crisis in Armenia and ongoing situation in Iraq where ancient indigenous non-Islamic peoples are also victims of jihad, and genocide because they do not follow Islam – sharia (8)(9).

> **Hamas Covenant 1988, Article Eleven:** "The Islamic Resistance Movement believes that the land of Palestine is an Islamic Waqf consecrated **for future Moslem generations** until Judgement Day. It, or any part of it, should not be squandered: it, or any part of it, should not be given up...

> This is the law governing the land of Palestine in the Islamic Sharia (law) and **the same goes for any land the Moslems have conquered by force**, because during the times of (Islamic) conquests, the Moslems consecrated these lands to Moslem generations till the Day of Judgement.

> This Waqf remains as long as earth and heaven remain. **Any procedure in contradiction to Islamic Sharia, where Palestine is concerned, is null and void**"(10).

Palestinians are free to enter - but for their own safety, Jewish residents are forbidden (11).

Sources:

(1) Waqf – modern guide:
https://guidingfriend.com/Waqf-board-land-property/

(2) 'Shari'ah Standards' The Accounting and Auditing Organization for Islamic Finance 2015. See Waqf - p.809-838
https://aaoifi.com/shariaa-standards/?lang=en#

(3) Hindustan Times
https://www.hindustantimes.com/india-news/in-tamil-nadu-Waqf-board-claims-ownership-of-an-entire-village-there-s-a-temple-too-101663245541768.html

(4) India Times:
https://www.indiatimes.com/explainers/news/what-is-waqf-act-and-who-owns-the-waqf-land-in-india-567556.html

(5) Map Ottoman Empire:

https://commons.wikimedia.org/wiki/Atlas_of_the_Ottoman_Empire#/media
/File:OttomanEmpireIn1683.png

(6) Israel Declaration Paragraph 13:

https://idi.theicenter.org/sites/default/files/Handout%203a-%20Israel%E2%80
%99s%20Declaration%20of%20Independence%20-%20English%20Translation/
index.pdf

(7) Grief, Howard, 'The Legal Foundation and borders of Israel under International Law' Mazo Pub 2011

(8) Armenia:

https://www.ncregister.com/cna/armenian-christians-trapped-and-facing-geno
cide-an-explainer

(9) Iraq:
https://www.bbc.com/news/world-middle-east-48333923

(10) Hamas Covenant:
https://avalon.law.yale.edu/20th_century/hamas.asp

(11) Oslo Accords (West Bank)
https://en.wikipedia.org/wiki/West_Bank_Areas_in_the_Oslo_II_Accord

RELEVANT DOCTRINE:

Koran 20.6 https://legacy.quran.com/20/6

Koran 13:41 https://legacy.quran.com/13/41

Hadith (Muslim 1632a) https://sunnah.com/muslim:1632a

Hadith (Bukhari 2772) https://sunnah.com/bukhari:2772

Hadith (Bukhari 2737) https://sunnah.com/bukhari:2737

Hadith (Bukhari 2313) https://sunnah.com/bukhari:2313

Hadith (Bukhari 3059) https://sunnah.com/bukhari:3059

Hadith (Bukhari 3012) https://sunnah.com/bukhari:3012

Hadith (Ibn Majah 2397) https://sunnah.com/ibnmajah:2397

CHAPTER TWENTY-ONE

JIHAD BY ANY OTHER NAME...

Is still jihad

"Hamas is not a national movement. Hamas is a religious movement with a goal to establish an Islamic state" (1)(2).

Question: Support for Hamas, a listed jihadi terrorist organization, has escalated in non-Islamic countries – how has this happened?

Answer: A general lack of knowledge regarding the contents of Islamic foundational doctrine and censorship of those who have knowledge but speak about it from the perspective of the non-Muslim.

Over half the Islamic foundational doctrine concerns the non-Muslim – so of course, they should know what it says. But most don't. They may have heard nice phrases that apply only to believers, but not heard the doctrine that applies to themselves.

An interesting exercise that anyone can perform to improve their knowledge is simply to search the word 'Jihad' in the Hadith and Koran using search engines such as these: Hadith (https://sunnah.com/) or Koran (https://legacy.quran.com/)

The opening chapter of the Koran 'al Fatiha' is a required prayer which is repeated up to 17 times a day:

- "Guide us to the Straight Way. The Way of those on whom You have bestowed Your Grace , not (the way) of those who earned Your Anger (*such as the Jews*), nor of those who went astray (*such as the Christians*)." [Koran 1:7, Khan translation]

This same prayer is often offered in Arabic at the start of 'Interfaith Dialogue' (Dawa) events while the non-Islamic participants, including Jews and Christians, naively smile and nod their approval believing that they have all just been blessed (3).

Jew hatred began a long time ago and is enshrined in, and sanctified by, Islamic doctrine. It stems from Mohammed's hope and expectation that the Jews of Medina would accept him as a prophet – but they did not. In only 5 years, all three tribes of Medina had either converted, been exiled or killed (4)(5)(6).

- "While we were in the Mosque, the Prophet came out and said, "Let us go to the Jews..." He said to them, "If you embrace Islam, you will be safe. You should know that the earth belongs to Allah and His Apostle, and I want to expel you from this land. So, if anyone amongst you owns some property, he is permitted to sell it, otherwise you should know that the Earth belongs to Allah and His Apostle." (Bukhari 3167)

Even in the 7thc. the power of having influencers on your side was known and utilized.

- Mohammed said: "Had only ten Jews (amongst their chiefs) believe me, all the Jews would definitely have believed me." (Bukhari 3941) And when he died Mohammed said 'expel the pagans from the Arabian peninsula and continue giving gifts to the foreign delegates as you have seen me dealing with them'. (Bukari 3053)

Mohammed also said:

- "War is deceit" (Bukhari 3029)

- "If I live - if Allah wills - I will expel the Jews and the Christians from the Arabian Peninsula." (Tirmidhi 1606)

- "The Hour will not be established until you fight with the Jews, and the stone behind which a Jew will be hiding will say. "O Muslim! There is a Jew hiding behind me, so kill him." (Bukhari 2926)

Even the trite became a command:

- "The Jews and the Christians do not dye their hair, so be different from them." (Bukhari 3462)

This is just a tiny fraction of what the doctrine says about the non-Muslim. Read it for yourself, reflect on what is happening now, and ask yourself - how could it be otherwise?

Sources :

(1) Hamas interview:
https://www.foxnews.com/media/son-hamas-leader-breaks-silence-decision-denounce-terror-group-care-palestinians

(2) Hamas in America:
https://extremism.gwu.edu/hamas-networks-america

(3) Al Fatiha prayer:
https://acdemocracy.org/what-are-praying-muslims-repeating-17-times-daily/

(4) Guillaume, Alfred. 'The Life of Muhammad: a Translation of Ishaq's Sirat Rasul Allah' (p. 231-232, 281, 363, 437, 461-66), Oxford University Press, 1982
https://archive.org/details/GuillaumeATheLifeOfMuhammad/page/n3/mode/2up

(5) Jew hatred in foundational Islamic doctrine:
https://www.cspii.org/learn-political-islam/methodology/statistical-analysis-political-islam/anti-jew-text-trilogy/

(6) Jew hatred in Koran:
https://cspi-web-media.ams3.cdn.digitaloceanspaces.com/documents/Jew_Hatred_Koran.pdf

RELEVANT DOCTRINE:

Koran 1:6-7 (Khan) https://legacy.quran.com/1/6-7

Hadith (Bukhari 3167) https://sunnah.com/bukhari:3167

Hadith (Muslim 2793) https://sunnah.com/muslim:2793

Hadith (Bukhari 3167) https://sunnah.com/bukhari:3941

Hadith (Bukhari 2926) https://sunnah.com/bukhari:2926

Hadith (Bukhari 2338) https://sunnah.com/bukhari:2338

Hadith (Bukhari 3122) https://sunnah.com/bukhari:3122

Hadith (Bukhari 3029) https://sunnah.com/bukhari:3029

CHAPTER TWENTY-TWO

ISLAM: POLITICAL OR RELIGIOUS?

– The educational solution for the non-Islamic state

A llahu Akbar has been the clarion call of jihad since its first utterance by Mohammed at Jewish Khaybar fourteen centuries ago. While humble Meccan caravans were the first targets of jihad, in the last month alone you can add Israel, Nigeria, Lebanon, Somalia, India, Pakistan, Philippines and many others to the list (1).

The history is well known. Mohammed began receiving revelations at age 40 and over the next 13 years gained approximately 150 followers. After his migration to Medina he picked up the sword, thus becoming a politician and jihadi – these days that is called a 'change of career' (2).

This new career brought with it incredible success in terms of numbers and booty. In fact, the entire eighth chapter of the Koran, revealed to Mohammed after the battle of Badr, is called 'The Spoils of War' describing how the spoils of war should be divided between Mohammed and his followers, particularly for those who fought.

During the last 9 years of his life, Mohammed was involved in a battle on an average of once every six and a half weeks as Islam expanded to encompass the entire Arabian peninsula (3). If an entire community simply acquiesced without fighting, then the tribute belonged entirely to Mohammed and Allah.

A steady income was also obtained from 'dhimmis', conquered people who were allowed to retain their beliefs but live under much reduced circumstances, be made to feel themselves 'subdued', pay as much as 50% of their income as 'jizya' for this protection, and liable to be routed at any time. (Koran 9:29)

Today, the Koran and Mohammed remain as the guiding lights of Islam and yet Islam is still referred to solely as a 'religion'.

For those who have been conquered over the centuries, up to and including the present day, not so much. Jihad continues as a threat in many non-Islamic countries and for their citizens, a source of genuine fear, not a phobia.

For this reason, it is time to take a closer look at how Islamic studies are vetted and taught in non-Islamic countries, who is teaching them, what they contain and how they are funded at every level.

In Europe and America, school books from the early grades present information about Islam in a very positive light that isn't necessarily historically accurate (4). Likewise, in North American universities, Islamic studies are frequently combined with activism promoting the concept of 'Islamophobia' with no representation for those who have been oppressed by Islamic regimes (5).

A new approach is overdue. Perhaps Political Science is the correct place to study the Political aspects of Islam, from a non-Islamic standpoint - after all, more than half of Islamic foundational doctrine is about the non-Muslim (6). The perspective of those who have been and are oppressed is also important, deserves study and a fair opportunity for academic representation and recognition.

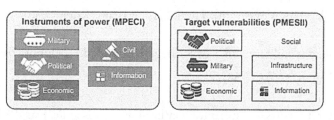

Figure 1.1 – MPECI instruments of power and PMESII target vulnerabilities

Factors Recommending Islam as a Political Entity:

- 31% of foundational Islamic doctrine is about jihad (7)(8)

- Countries are either Islamic or non-Islamic, as in communist or democratic

- The doctrine demonizes 'opposition' in the same way political parties often do

- The Organization of Islamic Co-operation (OIC) has 57 member states and forms the largest voting block at the U.N. (9)

- Political lobbying and activism by Islamic organizations – for example Canada's 'Special Representative to Combat Islamophobia, the 'Muslim Voting Guide 2019' and demands on non-Islamic governments at every level for changes to benefit Islam (10-14)

- Co-opting of National Institutions: Islamic banks and finance, the Liberal-Muslim Parliamentary caucus; Sharia 'courts' in the U.K. and E.U., Universities, Labour Unions, trade, political parties, judiciary, the Military (15-34)

- Islamophobia reports published annually by the OIC with recommendations that are in essence, political (35-36)

- Mandatory payment of 'zakat' (an Islamic tax) by all Muslims who are able. This is one of the 'Five Pillars' of Islam (Koran 9:60)

- Jihad is military and 1 of 8 categories entitled to support from Zakat (Koran 9:60) (37-38)

- Jihad persists in states until they become fully Islamic 'Dar al-Islam' (39)

- Jihad is often referred to in the doctrine as the 'best deed' rewarded with booty and if it results in death – then paradise. When Mohammed died, thousands tried to leave Islam resulting in the 'Ridda' (apostasy) wars and massive slaughter (40)

- Apostasy is forbidden and in the doctrine, warrants a death sentence. In non-Islamic countries apostates critical of Islam may be called Islamophobes. In Islamic states anyone critical of Islam may be killed as an apostate, or for blasphemy

- A person born Muslim has no choice in the matter

- The dualistic nature of Islam facilitates abusing non-violent Muslims as civilian shields, or as a Trojan horse for jihad. This is currently exemplified in Israel with jihadis using schools as munitions bases (41)(42)

- The stated goal of Islam is world domination (Ibn Majah 3952; Muslim 2889a)

- As previously non-Islamic states become Islamic, the existing social networks, traditions, structures and institutions from the 'period of ignorance' prior to Islam are destroyed and replaced with Islamic ones (43)

DISCUSSION:

The foregoing examples tick every box describing the '5 modes of entry' identified by the 2019 Multinational Capability Development Campaign (MCDC) as evidence of hybrid warfare (Figures 1 and 2). MCDC is a multinational initiative to address global security and prosperity (44).

Sharia, and Islamic instruments of power are to be expected in an Islamic state. However, in non-Islamic countries, the influence of sharia is also being exerted by utilizing various instruments of power to target vulnerabilities.

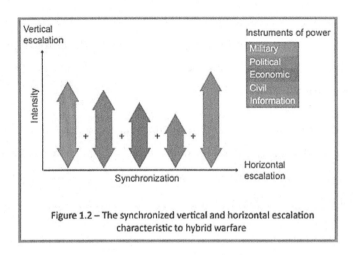

Figure 1.2 – The synchronized vertical and horizontal escalation characteristic to hybrid warfare

CONCLUSION:

So is Islam religious, or is it political, and how does a 'religion' retain such a designation? Should it have to pass some test, and should that test include a requirement that it does not demand the annihilation of those who do not submit or those who choose to leave Islam?

Perhaps the time has come to examine these questions carefully, and make haste to find the answers.

- Koran 9:14 "Fight them; Allah will punish them by your hands and will disgrace them and give you victory over them and satisfy the breasts of a believing people"

Sources:

(1) Jihad attacks last 30 days:
https://thereligionofpeace.com/attacks/attacks.aspx?Yr=Last30

(2) Guillaume, Alfred. 'The Life of Muhammad: a Translation of Ishaq's Sirat Rasul Allah'. Oxford University Press, 1967
https://archive.org/details/history-ibn-ishaq-sirat-rasul-allah-the-life-of-mu hammad/page/n7/mode/2up

(3) Ibid: (#973 p. 659-660)

(4) Sewall, Gilbert 'Islam in the Classroom' 2008:
https://files.eric.ed.gov/fulltext/ED501724.pdf

(5) Wilfred Laurier U.:
https://bridge.georgetown.edu/wp-content/uploads/2019/03/Canada-Fac tsheets-on-Islamophobia-Project-Language-1.pdf

(6) Statistical Analysis:
https://www.cspii.org/learn-political-islam/methodology/statistical-analysi s-political-islam/amount-text-devoted-kafir/

(7) Statistical Analysis:
https://www.cspii.org/learn-political-islam/methodology/statistical-analysi s-political-islam/trilogy-text-devoted-jihad/

(8) Battles of Mohammed:
https://www.wikiislam.net/wiki/List_of_expeditions_of_Muhammad

(9) OIC members:
https://www.oic-oci.org/states/?lan=en

(10) 'Special representative to combat Islamophobia'
https://toronto.citynews.ca/2023/01/26/nccm-combatting-islamophobia/

(11) Muslim Voting Guide:
https://torontosun.com/news/national/canadian-muslim-voting-guide-bre ached-federal-law-elections-commissioner

(12) Lobbying:
https://www.nccm.ca/wp-content/uploads/2022/08/NCCM-Islamophobi
a-Summit-1-Year-After-2022.pdf

(13) Canadian Summit:
https://www.nccm.ca/islamophobiasummit/

(14) Co-opting National Institutions: 'Countering Hybrid Warfare' 2017
p.9-10
https://assets.publishing.service.gov.uk/media/5a8228a540f0b62305b92ca
a/dar_mcdc_hybrid_warfare.pdf

(15) Canada Muslim Liberal Caucus:
https://capforcanada.com/new-muslim-liberal-party-caucus-speaks-to-the-f
uture-of-canadian-society/

(16) U.K. organizations:
https://en.wikipedia.org/wiki/Category:Islamic_organisations_based_in_t
he_United_Kingdom

(17) Finance:
https://thebanks.eu/articles/Islamic-banks-in-the-United-Kingdom

(18) Shariah mortgage:
https://torontosun.com/opinion/columnists/fatah-why-shariah-mortgage
-is-a-deception

(19) 'Shari'ah Standards' The Accounting and Auditing Organization for
Islamic Finance 2015 Sec 35 (9) p.897
https://aaoifi.com/shariaa-standards/?lang=en

(20) Trade: Halal Investing
https://woodgundyadvisors.cibc.com/web/khaled-sultan/halal-investing?la
ng=en_US

(21) Halal Expo:
https://halalexpocanada.com/index.html

(22) Education: Georgetown U.
https://bridge.georgetown.edu/about-us/

(23) Wilfred Laurier U.:
https://bridge.georgetown.edu/wp-content/uploads/2019/03/Canada-Fac
tsheets-on-Islamophobia-Project-Language-1.pdf

(24) Berkeley U.
https://crg.berkeley.edu/research/research-initiatives/islamophobia-researc
h-and-documentation-project

(25) Canada Elementary grades:
https://www.nccm.ca/wp-content/uploads/2022/01/EN-_GSC_Educatio
n_Material-1.pdf

(26) Labour Unions:
https://documents.clcctc.ca/human-rights-and-equality/islamophobia/Isla
mophobiaAtWork-Report-2019-03-20-EN.pdf

(27) Political parties:
https://jcpa.org/is-canadas-justin-trudeau-the-great-reformer-of-islam/

(28) National Summit:
https://www.canada.ca/en/canadian-heritage/news/2021/07/the-governme
nt-of-canada-concludes-national-summit-on-islamophobia.html

(29) Judiciary: UK Telegraph
https://www.telegraph.co.uk/politics/2023/10/28/mosque-chairman-prais
ed-hamas-leader-advises-cps/

(30) UK Crown Prosecution Service advised by Hamas supporter:
https://assets.publishing.service.gov.uk/government/uploads/system/uploads/a
ttachment_data/file/1134987/Independent_Review_of_Prevent__print_.pdf

(31) Canadian courts:
https://torontosun.com/opinion/columnists/fatah-shariah-law-makes-a-comeb
ack-in-ontario

(32) Military:
https://www.cbc.ca/news/canada/ottawa/canadian-military-seeks-muslim-recru
its-1.59939048

(33) UK Sharia Courts (Hansard):
https://hansard.parliament.uk/commons/2019-05-02/debates/201F2DB0-FC
E5-412F-AAB8-83CAA66F308A/ShariaLawCourts

(34) UK Sharia Courts (Parliamentary report):
https://researchbriefings.files.parliament.uk/documents/CDP-2019-0102/CD
P-2019-0102.pdf

(35) OIC Islamophobia reports:
https://www.oic-oci.org/page/?p_id=182&p_ref=61&lan=en

(36) U.N. Islamophobia action:
https://assembly.coe.int/LifeRay/EGA/Pdf/TextesProvisoires/2022/20220919
-AntiMuslimRacism-EN.pdf

(37) Military defn.
https://www.dictionary.com/browse/military

(38) Sharia, (Reliance of the Traveller h8.17, o9.1, o8.7(20)) Nuh Ha Mim Keller,
Amana Publications 2015
https://archive.org/details/relianceofthetravellertheclassicmanualofislamicsacre
dlaw

(39) Canada jihadi terrorists listed:
https://www.publicsafety.gc.ca/cnt/ntnl-scrt/cntr-trrrsm/lstd-ntts/crrnt-lstd-nt ts-en.aspx

(40) Ridda wars:
https://en.wikipedia.org/wiki/Ridda_Wars

(41) Civilian shield:
https://www.washingtonpost.com/news/morning-mix/wp/2014/07/31/why-h amas-stores-its-weapons-inside-hospitals-mosques-and-schools/

(42) Hamas:
https://www.zerohedge.com/geopolitical/hamas-leader-calls-global-muslim-up rising-day-rage-friday-report-says

(43) Buddhas destroyed:
https://www.nbcnews.com/news/world/taliban-destroyed-afghanistans-ancien t-buddhas-now-welcoming-tourists-rcna6307

(44) Multinational Capability Development Campaign (MCDC):
https://sites.apan.org/public/MCDCpub/Shared%20Documents/MCDC_Ov erview-20190530.pdf

Figures 1.1 & 1.2. Co-opting National Institutions: 'Countering Hybrid Warfare' MCDC 2019 (p.13-14) https://assets.publishing.service.gov.uk/government/uploads/system/uploads/a ttachment_data/file/784299/concepts_mcdc_countering_hybrid_warfare.pdf

RELEVANT DOCTRINE:

Koran Chapter 8 https://legacy.quran.com/8

Koran 98.6 https://legacy.quran.com/98/6

Koran 9:14 https://legacy.quran.com/9/14

Koran 13:41 https://legacy.quran.com/13/41

Koran 9:29 https://legacy.quran.com/9/29

Koran 2:216 https://legacy.quran.com/2/216

Koran 9:60 (Khan) https://legacy.quran.com/9/60

Hadith (Bukhari 947) https://sunnah.com/bukhari:947

Hadith (Bukhari 3152) https://sunnah.com/bukhari:3152

Hadith (Bukhari 610) https://sunnah.com/bukhari:610

Hadith (Bukhari 6922) https://sunnah.com/bukhari:6922

Hadith (Abu Dawud 4714) https://sunnah.com/abudawud:4714

Hadith (Bukhari 36) https://sunnah.com/bukhari:36

Hadith (Muslim 2889a) https://sunnah.com/muslim:2889a

Hadith (Bukhari 3167) https://sunnah.com/bukhari:3167

Hadith (Abu Dawud 2480) https://sunnah.com/abudawud:2480

Hadith (Muslim 523a) https://sunnah.com/muslim:523 a

Hadith (Bukhari 6098) https://sunnah.com/bukhari:6098

Hadith (Bukhari 6882) https://sunnah.com/bukhari:6882

Chapter Twenty-Three

What Mohammed Said...

M ohammed said "I have been sent with the shortest expressions bearing the widest meanings, and I have been made victorious with terror (cast in the hearts of the enemy) and while I was sleeping, the keys of the treasures of the world were brought to me and put in my hand." (Bukhari 2997)

There are many who dismiss this statement of Mohammed's saying that its equal can be found in the historical accounts of other beliefs and that 'religion' plays no part in Islamic jihad. Thus they dismiss the significance of a man whose life is so celebrated that a simple cartoon of him was paid for in lives (1)(2). A model of excellence that is unique to Islam.

- 'He who obeys the messenger, has obeyed Allah...' (Koran 4:80)

Is it surprising then that a recent survey of British Muslims found that just 23% say it would be undesirable to have Sharia law, 52% want to make it illegal to show a picture of Mohammed, and only 24% have a negative view of the designated Islamic terrorist organization Hamas? (3)

Just as Mohammed's military career progressed, so too did Islamic doctrine become ever more violent and earlier verses abrogated.

- "Muhammad is the Messenger of Allah; and those with him are forceful against the disbelievers, merciful among themselves..." (Koran 48:29)

When Mohammed and his followers took Mecca, all 360 idols in the Kaaba were destroyed and Koran 9:28 declares that 'unbelievers' must never again enter that city. Following this example, the Taliban destroyed the Buddhas of Afghanistan in 2001. They were declared to be 'un-Islamic' (4).

And yet it is the earlier Koranic verses that one hears in the public square – a disarmingly incomplete and hence deceptive picture. Even the obligatory veiling brutally imposed on women in Afghanistan (5) and Iran was not 'revealed' until 5 years after Mohammed's migration to Medina where women were instructed to "...abide in your houses and do not display yourself as the former times of ignorance.' (Koran 33:33). By then, Mohammed had already been preaching for 18 yrs.

Little wonder then that people are confused and believe that jihadis are 'extreme radicals'. An admission that such attacks demonstrate sincere devotion and a desire to attain a heavenly 'paradise' is simply too frightening to contemplate. (Bukhari 2787)

But it was only after jihad was adopted that Islam grew through conquest from 150 followers to encompass the entire Arabian peninsula. Sharia does not permit freedom of religion (commanding death to apostates Koran 4:89) or equality before the law (a woman's testimony is worth one-half a man's – Bukhari 304). Sharia is the ordained way of Islam – exemplified by the life of Mohammed.

What could be more significant than that?

For the last 9 years of his life Mohammed averaged a military expedition every 6.5 weeks and beheaded 600-900 Jews in a single day – the last of the three tribes of Medina who had thrived there only 5 years before (6).

Genuine fear is what religious minorities in many Islamic majority states live with as a matter of course and that same fear is now being felt in formerly peaceful Jewish neighbourhoods in non-Islamic countries (7)(8).

So yes, there is terror, and it's not 'phobic' (9). The doctrine commands it.

Study the doctrine.

Sources:

(1) BBC 2015:
https://www.bbc.com/news/world-europe-51018163

(2) BBC 2020:
https://www.bbc.com/news/world-europe-54632353

(3) Survey:
https://henryjacksonsociety.org/wp-content/uploads/2024/04/HJS-Deck-200324-Final.pdf

(4) Buddhas destroyed:
https://www.nbcnews.com/news/world/taliban-destroyed-afghanistans-ancient-buddhas-now-welcoming-tourists-rcna6307

(5) UK News:
https://www.dailymail.co.uk/news/article-13300915/British-Muslim-clerics-praise-beautiful-Taliban-true-freedom-felt-fact-finding-mission-Afghanistan.html

(6) Guillaume, Alfred. 'The Life of Muhammad: a Translation of Ishaq's Sirat Rasul Allah' (p. 281, 363, 437, 461-66, 659). Oxford University Press, 1967
https://archive.org/details/GuillaumeATheLifeOfMuhammad/page/n3/mode/2up

(7) Toronto Sun:
https://www.msn.com/en-ca/news/other/kinsella-is-this-at-long-last-the-result-of-multiculturalism/ar-BB1lzNdY

(8) Toronto Sun:
https://youtu.be/Ua9snxMgwIg

(9) U.N.Relief and Works Agency:
https://www.zerohedge.com/geopolitical/how-unrwa-grooms-terrorists

EDUCATIONAL VIDEO:
https://youtu.be/szQdhM2fFL4

Additional resources:
https://www.poi-nps.com/

RELEVANT DOCTRINE:

Hadith (Bukhari 2977) https://sunnah.com/bukhari:2977

Koran 2:106 https://legacy.quran.com/2/106

Koran 4:80 https://legacy.quran.com/4/80

Koran 9:28 https://legacy.quran.com/9/28

Koran 33:21 https://legacy.quran.com/33/21

Koran 33:33 https://legacy.quran.com/33/33

Koran 48:29 https://legacy.quran.com/48/29

CHAPTER TWENTY-FOUR

ARE THERE 3 ABRAHAMIC RELIGIONS?

And why is this concept being promoted?

There's been a lot of talk about 'the three Abrahamic religions' in the last couple of decades, fostered by 'Dialogue & Dawa' events, so let's have a closer look.

Mohammed began having revelations at the age of forty. This frightened him, he thought he might be mad or a poet, both of which he despised. His wife's Christian cousin was asked for help, and the cousin said that Mohammed must be a prophet (1).

Afterwards, Mohammed declared that the biblical prophets - Abraham, Noah, Moses etc. and Christ (Isa) were all born Muslim and that Mary, mother of Christ, was also the sister of Aaron (born 14 centuries earlier). Mohammed said that Christ was never crucified and that another was crucified in his place. This is not consistent with Judeo-Christian tradition.

During Mohammed's 'night journey to the farthest mosque (Jerusalem)' Islamic doctrine asserts that he was shown heaven, passing by Christ on the 2nd level and progressing to the highest 7th heaven (2). Mohammed also had a glimpse of hell, which he said contained mostly women who were ungrateful to their husbands. (Bukhari 304)

At first, Mohammed was not critical of Jews but after the migration (hijra) to Medina that changed.

The 3 Jewish tribes of Medina (half the population) did not accept Mohammed as prophet – within 5 years all 3 tribes were exiled or killed. Of the last tribe 600-900 men were beheaded in a single day, the women and children taken as captives and slaves (3).

Owing to the conflict between the Judeo/Christian texts and the Koran, Mohammed said that Christians and Jews, 'people of the book' corrupted their own scriptures, and that is what is taught to this very day. Mohammed sometimes granted them 'dhimmi' status – the right to pay a special tax called the 'jizya' and imposed many restrictions on them. If they paid it and felt themselves subdued, they were able to keep their lives. (Dawud 3006)

A few examples:

- Koran 2:159 Indeed, those who conceal what We sent down of clear proofs and guidance after We made it clear for the people in the Scripture, those are cursed by Allah and cursed by those who curse

- Koran 5:51 Oh believers, do not take the Jews or Christians as friends. They are but one another's friends. If any one of you take them for his friends, he surely is one of them

- Koran 3:54 ...Allah is the best of schemers

Perhaps more significant than similarities in the doctrine, are the differences. Christians and Jews study the old and new testaments and genealogies of the Bible. Islam uses the Koran and Sunna of Mohammed, the genealogy is questioned (4).

The example of Christ as recorded in the gospels, and that of Mohammed described in the Sira and Hadith, are diametrically opposed. For Islam, 'Believers' excludes those who do not follow Sharia, the way of Mohammed and Allah (5).

- Only Islam endorses and funds jihad through mandatory collection of zakat. (Koran 9:60)

- Only Islam says that Christ will return to destroy all religions except Islam. (Dawud 4324)

Dawa events (often called 'dialogues' or 'a common word') are meant to gain converts and support for Islam (6).

Look for original sources that have not been bowdlerized. They're a little tougher reading, but well worth the effort (7).

Sources:

(1) Guillaume, Alfred. 'The Life of Muhammad: a Translation of Ishaq's Sirat Rasul Allah' p106-107 (#153-154), Oxford University Press, 1967 (Ibn Ishaq 700-767CE) https://archive.org/details/history-ibn-ishaq-sirat-rasul-allah-the-life-of-muhammad/page/n7/mode/2up

(2) ibid p181-186 (#263-271)

(3) ibid p464 (#690-693)

(4) Amari, Dr. Rafat 'Is Mohammed a descendent of Ishmael?' from 'Islam in Light of History' https://web.archive.org/web/20231203080127/http://rrimedia.org/Resources/Articles/ArtMID/1379/ArticleID/53/Is-Mohammed-a-Descendant-of-Ishmael#_ednref14

(5) **EDUCATIONAL VIDEO**: 'Islam and the Unbelievers' https://www.youtube.com/watch?v=zNLEbDlHOOA&t=272s

(6) Siddiqi, Shamim, " Methodology of Dawah Elallah in American Perspective" Islamic Works Pub. 1989 http://www.dawahinamericas.com/bookspdf/Metho dologyofDawah.pdf

(7) Islamic doctrine (linked) https://www.poi-nps.com/

RELEVANT DOCTRINE:

Koran 2:59 https://legacy.quran.com/2/59

Koran 2:159 https://legacy.quran.com/2/159

Koran 3:54 https://legacy.quran.com/3/54

Koran 3:67 https://legacy.quran.com/3/67

Koran 4:157 https://legacy.quran.com/4/157

Koran 5:51 https://legacy.quran.com/5/51

Koran 8:12 https://legacy.quran.com/8/12

Koran 9:29 https://legacy.quran.com/9/29

Koran 9:60 https://legacy.quran.com/9/60

Koran 19:28-34 https://legacy.quran.com/19/28-34

Koran 27:76 https://legacy.quran.com/27/76

Hadith (Bukhari 304) https://sunnah.com/bukhari:304

Hadith (Dawud 4324) https://sunnah.com/abudawud:4324

Hadith (Dawud 2140) https://sunnah.com/abudawud:2140

Hadith (Muslim 2659a) https://sunnah.com/muslim:2659a

Hadith (Muslim 2405) https://sunnah.com/muslim:2405

CHAPTER TWENTY-FIVE

HOW DO YOU DEFINE HUMAN RIGHTS?

'**I**ranian Rapper sentenced to death for supporting anti-hijab protests' (1).

How do you define Human Rights? You might be surprised to discover that not everyone defines them the same way.

The Universal Declaration of Human Rights (2) was adopted by the United Nations in 1948 – there were 50 initial member states and Iran was one of them, as was Saudi Arabia. It may have been believed in 1948 that over time, all united nations would move towards the overarching principles enshrined in that Declaration. Article 1 states that 'All human beings are born free and equal in dignity and rights.'

That vision has not been realized, in fact many could argue that the reverse is true. For example, in spite of events such as the 'Rapper' – Mr. Salehi – mentioned above, Iran was recently appointed to chair a U.N. Human rights committee (3).

In 1990, the Organization of Islamic Cooperation (OIC) – adopted its own Declaration of Human Rights – the Cairo Declaration. Fifty-six members of the OIC are also members of the U.N. Articles 24 and 25 specifically stated that 'all rights and freedoms stipulated in this document are subject to Islamic Shari'ah', and that 'Islamic Shari'ah is the ONLY source of reference for explanation or clarification of any of the Articles' (4).

Over the last 3 decades, jihadist violence in Africa has escalated dramatically (5). There are now sharia courts to be found all over the U.K. and in 2019, the EU protested that:

- "Sharia councils provide alternative dispute resolution, whereby members of the Muslim community...often under considerable social pressure, accept their religious jurisdiction mainly in marital issues and Islamic divorce proceedings but also in matters relating to inheritance and Islamic commercial contracts. The Assembly is concerned that the rulings of the Sharia councils clearly discriminate against women in divorce and inheritance cases. The Assembly is aware that informal Islamic courts may also exist in other Council of Europe member States" (6).

In 2021, the revised 'Cairo Declaration' removed the word 'Shari'ah', replacing it with references to Islamic 'values and principles' as exemplified in the 'Charter of Medina' and the 'Last Sermon of Mohammed' which 'underpin the conception of human rights'. In other words, it is still Sharia (7).

The United Nation's Universal Declaration of Human Rights notes in the preamble that 'a common understanding of these rights and freedoms is of the greatest importance for the full realization of this pledge.' They could be forgiven for believing in 1948 that this pledge would be worked towards by all parties but the OIC has since adopted an entirely different pledge from that of the United Nations – one that follows Sharia.

As these two Declarations of Human Rights are diametrically opposed one can only ask which one will succeed and why is it that some member states can, in good conscience, subscribe to both?

Sources:

EDUCATIONAL VIDEO: Universal Declaration of Human Rights vs Cairo Declaration at the U.N.
https://youtu.be/ZhkeVN26Go0

(1) News France
https://www.france24.com/en/asia-pacific/20240424-iran-sentences-popular-rapper-to-death-for-supporting-mahsa-amini-protests

(2) Universal Declaration of Human Rights:
https://www.ohchr.org/sites/default/files/UDHR/Documents/UDHR_Translations/eng.pdf

(3) News Reuters
https://www.reuters.com/world/irans-appointment-chair-un-rights-meeting-draws-condemnation-2023-11-02/

(4) Cairo Declaration 1990
https://elearning.icrc.org/detention/en/story_content/external_files/Human%20Rights%20in%20Islam%20(1990).pdf

(5) Africa Center for Strategic Studies
https://africacenter.org/spotlight/fatalities-from-militant-islamist-violence-in-africa-surge-by-nearly-50-percent/

(6) Sharia, the Cairo Declaration and the European Convention of Human Rights (Resolution 2253 2019)
https://assembly.coe.int/nw/xml/XRef/Xref-XML2HTML-en.asp?fileid=25353

(7) Cairo Declaration 2021
https://www.oic-oci.org/upload/pages/conventions/en/CDHRI_2021_ENG.pdf

Chapter Twenty-Six

International Women's Day May Be Replaced By...

World Hijab Day?

What is the difference between a woman and a veil?

Absolutely nothing by some standards – but for the rest of us, why would we choose to celebrate a piece of clothing rather than the human being wearing it? And do the people who choose to celebrate 'World Hijab Day' know much about the hijab – or are they jumping on the bandwagon without giving it much thought.

Six years ago women in Pakistan began the 'Aura March' on International Women's Day to bring attention to the desperate plight of women in that country. Not to be outdone, in 2022, religious leaders in Pakistan called for replacing International Women's Day with 'International Hijab Day' (1)(2).

Rather than supporting these women over the demands of the religious leaders, Canada started 'Celebrating World Hijab Day' in its schools several years ago demonstrating a rather myopic view in two ways (3):

1. The idea of 'celebrating' conveys a positive spin that cannot fail to affect impressionable young minds, and

2. 'Celebrating' fails to accurately reflect that where sharia is strictly enforced, the hijab is compulsory and women have little reason to celebrate. This can happen to women anywhere, not just in Islamic countries.

For some, the idea of veiled women may conjure up 'Tales of Arabian Nights', for others a fashion craze being sported by TikTok influencers (4) or a fun event at school - allegedly to encourage multiculturalism but often presenting a very one sided view of the subject (5)(6).

For others, the veil is none of these things.

- Koran 33:59 O Prophet, tell your wives and your daughters and the women of the believers to bring down over themselves [part] of their outer garments. That is more suitable *that they will be known and not be abuse*d. And ever is Allah Forgiving and Merciful.

- Hadith: Bukhari 146 "...So Allah revealed the verses of "Al-Hijab" (A complete body cover excluding the eyes)."

Rather than joining with the religious leaders in Pakistan or Iran, perhaps we can give some thought to the hijab not as it is portrayed in fashion magazines and fairy tales, but how it is experienced by women who dare not resist the doctrinal obligation to wear it. One-hundred thousand women marched against wearing the hijab in 1979 Iran, but 45 years later they, and their female children, are still forced to comply owing to sharia (7). Cameras have been installed to ensure compliance (8). The same is true for women in Afghanistan, they have no choice and many have died as a result (9).

So let's step out of our comfort zone and talk about the less attractive aspects of the hijab on International Women's Day, and the day after and the next. And remember it is the person wearing the clothing that matters, not the cloth.

To learn about the hijab from its inception to present day, please watch this video and share it with your friends on International Women's Day or any other day. Knowledge and a willingness to communicate that knowledge is how we can support those women who are compelled to wear the veil no matter where they live.

EDUCATIONAL VIDEO: Unveiling the mystery
https://www.youtube.com/watch?v=ZIq0tYiSVjA&t=28s

Sources:

(1) Pakistan 2022:
https://www.malaysiasun.com/news/272321700/pakistan-religious-affairs-minister-appeals-to-imran-khan-to-declare-women-day-as-international-hijab-day

(2) Pakistan 2023:
https://thefridaytimes.com/08-Mar-2023/another-women-s-day-in-pakistan-but-where-do-women-stand

(3) Canada 2024:
https://www.vsb.bc.ca/_ci/p/70620

(4) Roy, Jessica 'On TikTok, an Unlikedly Call to Islam Emerges' New Line Magazine Dec.1, 2023
https://newlinesmag.com/reportage/on-tiktok-an-unlikely-call-to-islam-emergs/

(5) Vancouver School Celebrates 'World Hijab Day'
https://www.vsb.bc.ca/_ci/p/70620

(6) Press Release 'World Hijab Day'
https://worldhijabday.com/12th-annual-whd-press-release/

(7) Iran 1979:
https://rarehistoricalphotos.com/women-protesting-hijab-1979/

(8) Iran 2023:
https://www.bbc.com/news/world-65220595

(9) Afghanistan 2024:
https://news.un.org/en/story/2024/02/1146177

RELEVANT DOCTRINE:

Koran 4:34 https://legacy.quran.com/24/31

Koran 24:31 https://legacy.quran.com/24/31

Koran 33:33 https://legacy.quran.com/33/33

Koran 33:59 https://legacy.quran.com/33/59

Hadith (Bukhari 146) https://sunnah.com/bukhari:146

Hadith (Bukhari 372) https://sunnah.com/bukhari:372

Hadith (Bukhari 5825) https://sunnah.com/bukhari:5825

Hadith (Dawud 641) https://sunnah.com/abudawud:641

CHAPTER TWENTY-SEVEN

'GAYS FOR GAZA'

- Useful till they aren't

"Gays for Gaza" protesters are an unhappy reminder of how poorly informed citizens of non-Islamic states are regarding the foundational doctrine of Islam (1). Members of the LGBTQ+ community carrying these banners show a distinct lack of self-preservation in their determination to ignore warnings that for them, living in an Islamic country could bring a death sentence (2)(3).

In Israel, homosexuals are protected by law and even at that, in 2022, a gay man from Gaza fled to Israel for safety but was kidnapped, brought back to Hebron and beheaded there (4)(5). During ISIS reign in the Middle East, homosexuals were routinely thrown off rooftops and stoned to death (6).

Politicians are also misinformed. For example in 2022, the Canadian government donated $687,000 to the Islamic Society of North America (ISNA) towards building an Islamic Centre at Yellowknife, NWT (7). It is well known that the then Prime Minister of Canada strongly supported the gay community (8). and yet a previous president of ISNA clearly stated that "Being gay and Muslim is a contradiction in terms. Islam is totally against homosexuality. It's clear in the Koran and in the sayings of the prophet Mohammed" (9).

Of course this is nothing new, so why are people in non-Islamic countries not better educated? Inadequate and 'Islamophobia conscious' schooling on the subject of Islam is a contributing factor (10) but also deliberate dissimulation.

In 2016, a self-proclaimed U.S. born jihadi shot 49 people at the homosexual PULSE nightclub in Orlando Florida. Publicly, Western Islamic leaders quickly denounced the shooting (11) while at the same time privately supporting Islamic groups that regularly host speakers condemning the gay community (12).

Visiting Islamic lecturers may also be found advocating for violence against homosexuality in countries far from recognized 'hotbeds' of civil unrest (13).

Islam's view on the LGBTQ+ community is best served by studying the Islamic Doctrine itself and understanding the imperative to follow it or be accused of apostasy (14). Here are just a few examples:

- Homosexuality is a grave sin which violates the will of Allah. Such behaviour is worse than any other sexual sin and degrades not only the individuals involved but those around them. (Koran 7:80-81)

- Homosexuals are cursed. Indeed, not only homosexuals are cursed but also effeminate men and masculine women, men who wear women's clothing and women who wear men's. Turn them out of your houses. (Hadith Bukhari 5886)

- Homosexuals can be killed. Execution or punishment may take the form of stoning, scourging, being blinded or in the case of lesbians, confined to the house until they die. (Koran 54:37, Koran 4:15, Koran 24:2, Hadith Dawud 4462)

- Homosexuals can be killed whether they are Muslim or not (15).

Please review the sources and discover the doctrine for yourself.

Sources:

(1) **EDUCATIONAL VIDEO**: 'Gays for Gaza'
https://www.bitchute.com/video/bctK9l41pyHT/

(2) Map of countries that criminalize:
https://www.humandignitytrust.org/lgbt-the-law/map-of-criminalisation/?typ
e_filter_submitted=&type_filter%5B%5D=crim_lgbt

(3) U.S. Commission Fact Sheet:
https://www.uscirf.gov/sites/default/files/2021-03/2021%20Factsheet%20-%20
Sharia%20and%20LGBTI.pdf

(4) UK Magazine:
https://quillette.com/2023/11/02/queers-for-palestine/

(5) Jerusalem Post:
https://www.jpost.com/middle-east/article-719063?ref=quillette.com

(6) NBC News:
https://www.nbcnews.com/storyline/isis-uncovered/isis-hurls-gay-men-buildin
gs-stones-them-analysts-n305171

(7) Canada funds ISNA centre:
https://www.cbc.ca/news/canada/north/yellowknife-islamic-centre-constructio
n-summer-2023-1.6635657

(8) Canada Magazine:
https://savethewest.com/lgbtq-the-islamic-perspective-canada/

(9) U.S. News:
https://www.sfgate.com/news/article/Gay-Muslims-battle-oppression-Support
-network-2906320.php

(10) The Telegraph:
https://web.archive.org/web/20220412132831/https://www.telegraph.co.uk/
world-news/2021/11/24/school-pulls-event-former-islamic-state-sex-slave-fears
-would/

(11) Time Magazine:
https://time.com/4365689/orlando-shooting-muslim-nightclub/

(12) Middle East Forum:
https://www.meforum.org/6069/cair-doesnt-like-homosexuals

(13) German News:
https://www.dw.com/en/germany-expels-openly-homophobic-imam/a-651049
4

(14) News video:
https://www.bitchute.com/video/BMOv7mlp9jbn/

(15) Sharia (Reliance of the Traveller a4.6, o12.1-2, p17.1-3, p28.1(2-3)) Umdat
al-Salik trans by Nuh Ha Mim Keller, Amana Publications 2015
https://archive.org/details/relianceofthetravellertheclassicmanualofislamicsacre
dlaw

RELEVANT DOCTRINE:

Koran 4:15 https://legacy.quran.com/4/15

Koran 7:80-81 https://legacy.quran.com/7/80-81

Koran 24:2 (Khan) https://legacy.quran.com/24/2

Koran 26:165-168 https://legacy.quran.com/26/165-168

Koran 29:28-29 https://legacy.quran.com/29/28-29

Koran 54:36-37 https://legacy.quran.com/54/36-37

Hadith (Dawud 4462) https://sunnah.com/abudawud:4462

Hadith (Dawud 4463) https://sunnah.com/abudawud:4463

Hadith (Bukhari 5886) https://sunnah.com/bukhari:5886

Hadith (Bukhari 6922) https://sunnah.com/bukhari:6922

Hadith (Nasa'i 5659) https://sunnah.com/nasai:5659

CHAPTER TWENTY-EIGHT

WHEN IS 'COURTESY' A BRIDGE TOO FAR?

"Twenty Four children were told they could not drink water at a school in Germany because three other students in the class were Muslims observing Ramadan, according to a report" (1).

Of course, this outrages non-Muslims. Why should the traditions of one belief system be permitted to impact in a negative way on those who do not follow it? The article then goes on to say that:

'A father of one of the students noted "We found this announcement strange...the children in fifth grade are between 10 and 11 years old. Even for religious Muslims, the fasting requirement only applies from the age of 14."'

That is not actually correct and in a non-Islamic state, no teacher should be enforcing sharia on anyone.

Islamic foundational doctrine declares that all are born 'fitra' (Muslim) and that it is our parents who 'corrupt us': Mohammed said, "No child is born except on Al-Fitra (Islam) and then his parents make him Jewish, Christian or Magian, as an animal produces a perfect young animal: do you see any part of its body amputated?..." (Bukhari 4775)

Sharia itself is not a collection of laws, it is the 'ordained way of Islam' in its entirety, but in 'Reliance of the Traveller' (2) (a handbook of sharia) we find these specifics about who is expected to fast:

---

i1.0 FASTING RAMADAN "Islam is built upon five: testifying there is no god but Allah and that Muhammad is the messenger of Allah, performing the prayer, giving zakat, making the pilgrimage to the House [Kaaba], and fasting Ramadan.")

il.l Fasting Ramadan is obligatory for:

(a) EVERY MUSLIM (0: male or female) who:

(b) HAS REACHED PUBERTY;

(e) and if female, is not in the period of menstruation or postnatal bleeding (nifas).

i1.2 The following are not required to fast:

(2) (non-b) a child;

i1.3 The following are not required to fast, though they are obliged to make up fast-days missed

(1) those who are ill

(2) those who are travelling

(3) A PERSON WHO HAS LEFT ISLAM

i1.5 A child of seven is ordered to fast, and at ten is beaten for not fasting (N: with the reservations mentioned at f1.2)."

Learning about Islam and its effect on other cultures is time well spent for those who wish to resist the Islamisation of their country. Expecting non-Muslims to accommodate or even comply with the requirements of sharia out of 'courtesy' is one of the several ways in which a non-Islamic state is, over time, transformed into an Islamic one.

Sources:

(1) ZeroHedge:
https://www.zerohedge.com/political/10-year-old-kids-denied-drinking-water-class-because-three-muslims-observing-ramadan

(2) Reliance of the Traveller (i1.1-5) Umdat al-Salik trans by Nuh Ha Mim Keller, Amana Publications 2015 (Sharia)
https://archive.org/details/relianceofthetravellertheclassicmanualofislamicsacredlaw

EDUCATIONAL VIDEO: Islam and the Unbelievers: Christians, Jews and Others'
https://youtu.be/zNLEbDlHOOA

RELEVANT DOCTRINE:

Koran 2:183 https://legacy.quran.com/2/183

Hadith (Bukhari 4775) https://sunnah.com/bukhari:4775

CHAPTER TWENTY-NINE

WHAT HAS HAPPENED TO ENGLAND?

Well, things certainly have changed in 'Merry Olde England' over the last couple of decades. Along with escalating antisemitism (1) Whitehall's 'Civil Service Muslim Network' has "directed officials to a website on which homosexuality is described as a "scourge" and "western modernity" likened to a "disease" (2).

This same 'cross-government group which represents and supports Muslim officials' was recently suspended for its anti-Semitic innuendos and evident support for the Oct 7th jihadi attack against civilians in Israel.

What we're really talking about here is tolerance. Everyone recognizes that lack of tolerance can be carried to extremes but so too can tolerance. To be tolerant of intolerance is to be complicit – one is as bad as the other. It is not for any minority group to take advantage of a tolerant society and abuse the rights they have been afforded there.

Shunning, attacking or otherwise mistreating homosexuals is something one can expect in an Islamic State because it is in accordance with the foundational Islamic doctrine:

- "Do you approach males among the worlds And leave what your Lord has created for you as mates? But you are a people transgressing." (Koran 26:165-166)

In Saudi Arabia, schoolbooks proclaim that the punishment for homosexuality is death – "both the active and passive participants are to be killed" and offer many Koranic references by way of confirmation (3). Non-compliance is not an option:

- "When Allah and His Messenger have decided a matter, no believer, male or female, has a choice in their affair" (Koran 33:36)

But amongst non-Islamic countries, not only England is having these issues. In Canada, Western University was forced to remove a poster showing two girls in hijabs kissing owing to backlash from the Islamic Community (4).

In Islam, lesbianism between women is considered adultery. Sharia demands the death sentence for adulterers. Mohammed cursed effeminate men and those women who assume the mannerisms of men, and said to "turn them out of your houses" (Bukhari 5886). As above, there is little choice.

Choosing to leave Islam – apostasy – is similarly punished. All roads lead to the same destination (Bukhari 6878).

Adhering to the ordained way of Islam, Sharia, is a communal obligation: "And let there be from you a nation inviting to good, enjoining what is right and forbidding what is wrong, and those will be the successful" (Koran 3:104). That is, the right and wrong as defined by sharia.

In 2021, The U.S. Commission on Religious Freedom wrote:

- 'In countries that rely on Sharia principles, "individuals suspected of violating laws against LGBTI activity are often victims of mob justice, with human rights organizations accusing the government of complicity and willful impunity for the perpetrators"' (5).

Minorities of all kinds, including religious minorities (6), women and children (7), enjoy rights, and protections in non-Islamic states that are not afforded by sharia. Accommodating sharia can only result in a lessening of those protections (8). We would do well to remember that and act accordingly.

Sources:

(1) Reuters:
https://www.reuters.com/world/uk/uk-records-worst-year-antisemitism-after-outbreak-israel-hamas-war-2024-02-15/

(2) UK News:
https://www.msn.com/en-us/news/world/civil-service-guidance-directed-officials-to-website-that-likened-homosexuality-to-a-scourge/ar-BB1k106T

(3) Saudi School books:
https://web.archive.org/web/20110808065439/https://www.hudson.org/files/pdf_upload/Excerpts_from_Saudi_Textbooks_715.pdf

(4) Canada News:
https://lfpress.com/news/local-news/western-university-lgbtq-poster-sparks-muslim-community-backlash

(5) U.S. Fact Sheet:
https://www.uscirf.gov/sites/default/files/2021-03/2021%20Factsheet%20-%20Sharia%20and%20LGBTI.pdf

(6) Newsweek:
https://www.newsweek.com/turkeys-christians-face-increasingly-dangerous-persecution-opinion-1583041

(7) Greek News Taliban:
https://greekreporter.com/2021/08/26/what-sharia-law-how-does-affect-women/

(8) Sharia, the Cairo Declaration and the European Convention of Human Rights (Resolution 2253 2019)
https://assembly.coe.int/nw/xml/XRef/Xref-XML2HTML-en.asp?fileid=253 53

RELEVANT DOCTRINE:

Koran 26:165-166 https://legacy.quran.com/26/165-166

Koran 33:36 https://legacy.quran.com/33/36

Koran 3:104 https://legacy.quran.com/3/104

Hadith (Bukhari 5886) https://sunnah.com/bukhari:5886

Hadith (Bukhari 6878) https://sunnah.com/bukhari:6878

Hadith (Nasa'i 5659) https://sunnah.com/nasai:5659

CHAPTER THIRTY

BLASPHEMY OR 'ISLAMOPHOBIA' – A QUESTION OF DEGREE, OR A MATTER OF TIME?

One hundred and sixty Christians were slaughtered by Islamic jihadis in Nigeria over the 2023 Christmas weekend (1).

Where are the protests? Where are the headlines? Such horrific events are so common now in Nigeria you'd expect people everywhere to be rising in anger, but they are not. Why not?

Earlier in the year, a young Christian student in Nigeria was stoned to death on university premises and her corpse burned while the perpetrators filmed the event. Her crime? Blasphemy,

And how was blasphemy defined on that occasion? A 'WhatsApp' post criticizing her classmates use of their study group to discuss Islamic ideology rather than academic themes (2).

Islamophobes are characterized as "phobic" i.e. mentally ill, racist, or religious bigots. Does that sound right? Or, is fear of Islam entirely rational given the never ending parade of jihadi attacks around the globe that happen on almost a daily basis? (3)

Perhaps most Islamophobes are in fact, not only rational but well informed, compassionate people concerned for the welfare of those currently suffering under 'blasphemy' laws and alarmed at the steady growth of Islamic organizations and incremental but effective implementation of sharia in secular bodies and states such as Nigeria where "Most blasphemy accusations are made by Muslims against Christians and frequently trigger mob violence before any official actions like police arrests and judicial trials can be taken" (4).

In 2023, a Canadian man was accused of being an Islamophobe and fired from his job for writing, in a 2009 book review, that 'it is the history of Islam that informs the jihadis of today'. Considering that jihadis frequently shout 'Khaybar, Khaybar' or 'Allahu Akbar' – significant events in Islamic history – his review would appear to be entirely reasonable (5).

After all, Sharia is contrary to the Universal Code of Human Rights (6).

Sharia permits stoning, amputation, child marriage, and death to apostates:

- "whoever changed his Islamic religion, then kill him' to name just a few.(Bukhari 6922)

In Canada, hate crimes against Jews between 2018 and 2021 were 18 times higher per capita than against the Islamic community and have continued to escalate. Yet Canada recognizes an 'Action against Islamophobia' day and has a special representative to combat Islamophobia (7)(8).

I am reminded of the child's story 'The Emperor's new clothes' – where only a naïve child, unaware of potential consequences such as losing your job or your life, dared to say 'The Emperor has no clothes!' Apparently the situation had not yet progressed to the point he would be incinerated for speaking truth like that young Nigerian girl, but isn't that where the West is headed?

Blasphemy laws might best be described as 'Islamophobia' laws minus the training wheels (9). Whether the terror is directed at students (10), Jewish businesses and synagogues (11)(12), apostates (13) or Christians (14), the question of 'degree' is really only a matter of time.

Sources:

(1) U.S. News:
https://gellerreport.com/2023/12/genocide-muslims-slaughter-another-160-ch ristians-preparing-for-church-christmas-programs-in-nigeria.html/?lctg=10374 4783

(2) CNN:
https://www.cnn.com/2022/05/13/africa/female-student-blasphemy-attack-in tl/index.html

(3) Wikipedia:
https://en.wikipedia.org/wiki/Lynching_of_Deborah_Yakubu

(4) Jihad attacks:
https://www.thereligionofpeace.com/attacks/attacks.aspx?Yr=Last30

(5) Canada News:
https://www.cbc.ca/news/canada/calgary/collin-may-human-rights-commission -shandro-lawsuit-1.6605527

(6) Universal Declaration of Human Rights:
https://www.ohchr.org/sites/default/files/UDHR/Documents/UDHR_Trans lations/eng.pdf

(7) Chart: Statistics Canada 'Number of police-reported hate crimes motivated by religion, Canada, 2018 to 2021'
https://www150.statcan.gc.ca/n1/daily-quotidien/230322/cg-a004-eng.htm

(8) Canada Announcement:
https://www.pm.gc.ca/en/news/news-releases/2023/01/26/prime-minister-ann ounces-appointment-canadas-first-special

(9) Blasphemy laws upheld:
https://www.reuters.com/world/africa/nigerias-sharia-blasphemy-law-not-unconstitutional-court-rules-2022-08-17/

(10) U.S. News:
https://www.usatoday.com/story/news/politics/2023/11/20/rising-antisemitism-campus-federal-investigation/71579893007/

(11) Canada News:
https://montrealgazette.com/news/local-news/jewish-owned-businesses-in-montreal-targeted-with-antisemitic-profanity

(12) The Gazette:
https://montrealgazette.com/news/local-news/west-island-synagogue-jewish-community-centre-firebombed-montreal-police-say

(13) Apostasy Q&A:
https://islamqa.info/en/answers/811/why-death-is-the-punishment-for-apostasy

(14) ACN News:
https://acninternational.org/anti-christian-violence-in-nigeria/

RELEVANT DOCTRINE:

Koran 5:33 https://legacy.quran.com/5/33

Koran 6:93 https://legacy.quran.com/6/93

Koran 33:57 https://legacy.quran.com/33/57

Koran 33:61 https://legacy.quran.com/33/61

Koran 65:1-4 https://legacy.quran.com/65/1-4

Hadith (Muslim Bk 2, 146) https://sunnah.com/muslim:1801

Hadith (Nasa'i 4059) https://sunnah.com/nasai:4059

Hadith (Bukhari 6922) https://sunnah.com/bukhari:6922

Hadith (Bukhari 2314) https://sunnah.com/bukhari:2314

Hadith (Bukhari 6930) https://sunnah.com/bukhari:6930

Hadith (Dawud 4324) https://sunnah.com/abudawud:4324

CHAPTER THIRTY-ONE

CANADIAN GOVERNMENT ANNOUNCES 'HALAL MORTGAGES'

What does that mean for this country – or any other?

People think there is no sharia in Canada. They are wrong, there is a great deal. CIBC – a chartered Canadian bank - currently partners with Wood Gundy to provide halal investment opportunities described as 'socially responsible and ethical investing' (1).

Canada hosts the largest halal expo in North America every year featuring a host of products and services. Expo 2024 boasts "From Food and Beverage, to Pharmaceuticals, to Cosmetics, from Finance to E-commerce and Logistics to Tourism and more, the entire halal industry will gather under one roof providing traders and buyers with the ideal platform to network and share market insights" (2).

The halal certification market also contributes to and promotes Sharia, affecting not only finance but ultimately restricting employment opportunities for non-Muslims (3)(4). Sharia is all encompassing, affecting virtually every aspect of life – including trade and commerce (5).

All halal investment vehicles must have a Sharia Board and are obligated to follow Sharia law. Sharia is inconsistent with the Universal Declaration of Human Rights. It does not recognize freedom of religion, or equality before the law. In addition, all profits and fees will be subject to 'zakat' - the Islamic tax. This tax has eight categories for disbursement – the seventh is jihad, which Sharia describes as a 'communal obligation':

- Koran 9:60 "As-Sadaqat (here it means Zakat) are only for the Fuqara' (poor), and Al-Masakin (the poor) and those employed to collect (the funds); and for to attract the hearts of those who have been inclined (towards Islam); and to free the captives; and for those in debt; **and for Allah's Cause (i.e. for Mujahidun - those fighting in the holy wars)**, and for the wayfarer (a traveller who is cut off from everything); a duty imposed by Allah. And Allah is All-Knower, All-Wise" (6).

- "09.1 Jihad is a communal obligation (def: c3.2). When enough people perform it to successfully accomplish it, it is no longer obligatory upon others (0: the evidence for which is the Prophet's saying (Allah bless him and give him peace), "He who provides the equipment for a soldier in jihad has himself performed jihad," and Allah Most High having said: (7)

  ○ "Those of the believers who are unhurt but sit behind are not equal to those who fight in Allah's path with their property and lives. Allah has preferred those who fight with their property and lives a whole degree above those who sit behind. And to each. Allah has promised great good"" (Koran 4:95)

There is no reason to provide halal mortgages because the Islamic principle of Darura applies today just as it always has (8):

- "He has only forbidden to you dead animals, blood, the flesh of swine, and that which has been dedicated to other than Allah . But **whoever is forced [by necessity], neither desiring [it] nor transgressing [its limit], there is no sin upon him**. Indeed, Allah is Forgiving and Merciful" (Koran 2:173)

The principle of Darura is why Muslims have no problem taking out an ordinary mortgage in a non-Islamic country (if there are no halal mortgages available) and have done so without hardship for decades: 'Necessity overcomes obligation'. However, once a halal mortgage is available, Muslims may be pressured by entities within the Islamic community, the 'Ummah', to use a halal mortgage instead of a conventional one whether they want to or not (9)(10)(11).

Promoting sharia mortgages in a non-Islamic country introduces Sharia law in a very substantial way. Non-Muslims will also be urged to invest in 'ethical mortgages' - this is the language that is used - and they may do so to encourage 'multiculturalism'. Many Canadians have adopted this blanket attitude without thoroughly investigating exactly what it is they are supporting and would be shocked to discover what having a 'Sharia board' actually means.

Sharia is already far advanced in the United Kingdom including food, finance, insurance, schools, courts, sharia compliant regulations enforced in hospitals and other public institutions and more. What is left before the U.K. becomes fully Sharia compliant? Only time.

Canada has long had a reputation as a safe haven for people seeking asylum. This includes Coptic Christians, Christians, Hindus, Zoroastrians, Baha'i, Jews, apostates and other minorities fleeing Islamic regimes. They are seeing more and more capitulation to demands for Sharia in this country and it is alarming.

Sources:

(1) CIBC halal investments
https://woodgundyadvisors.cibc.com/web/khaled-sultan/halal-investing

(2) Canada Halal Expo
https://halalexpocanada.com/index.html

(3) Solomon, Sol 'Islamisation through Halal products'
https://archive.christianconcern.com/sites/default/files/20190114_ChristianC
oncern_PolicyReport_HalalFoods.pdf

(4) Florence Bergeaud-Blackler et al 'Islam, politics and markets in global perspective' 2015

(5) **EDUCATIONAL VIDEO**: What is Sharia?
https://youtu.be/szQdhM2fFL4

(6) 'Shari'ah Standards' The Accounting and Auditing Organization for Islamic Finance 2017, Sec 35 (9) p 896
https://aaoifi.com/shariaa-standards/?lang=en

(7) Reliance of the Traveller Nuh Ha Mim Keller, Amana Publications 2015 (o9.1)
https://archive.org/details/relianceofthetravellertheclassicmanualofislamicsacre
dlaw

(8) Oxford Reference (darura):
https://www.oxfordreference.com/display/10.1093/oi/authority.20110810104
722491

(9) Sookhdeo, Dr. Patrick 'Understanding Shari'a Finance' Isaac Pub. 2008 (p.7
8-79)

(10) News: Court decision supports sharia
https://torontosun.com/opinion/columnists/fatah-shariah-law-makes-a-comeb
ack-in-ontario

(11) News: Shariah Mortgages:
https://torontosun.com/opinion/columnists/fatah-why-shariah-mortgage-is-a
-deception

RELEVANT DOCTRINE:

Koran 9:60 https://legacy.quran.com/9/60 (Zakat Tax)

Koran 2:173 https://legacy.quran.com/2/173 (Darura)

Reliance of the Traveller Nuh Ha Mim Keller, Amana Publications 2015 (o9. 1) https://archive.org/details/relianceofthetravellertheclassicmanualofislamicsa credlaw

CHAPTER THIRTY-TWO

WHAT WAS 'THE HOLY LAND FOUNDATION'?

S hort answer – a conspiracy to underwrite Hamas's campaign against Israel and the subject of the largest Hamas and Jihadi financing case ever successfully prosecuted in the U.S. concluding in November 2008 with convictions and lengthy prison terms on 108 counts.

From its inception, the Holy Land Foundation (HLF) existed to support Hamas and its goal of creating an Islamic Palestinian State by eliminating the State of Israel through violent Jihad. Before HLF was identified as a 'Specially Designated Terrorist' organization by the Treasury Department and shut down in December 2001, it was the largest U.S. Muslim charity.

After 1995, when it first became illegal to provide financial support to Hamas, HLF nevertheless provided approximately $12.4 million in funding. The government's case included testimony that in the early 1990's, Hamas' parent organization, the Muslim Brotherhood, planned to establish a network of organizations in the U.S. to spread a militant message and raise money for Hamas. The government's case also included testimony about Hamas material found in zakat committees.(zakat is the compulsory Islamic tax sometimes called 'Islamic charity' and is a pillar of Islam.) The defendants sent HLF-raised funds to Hamas-controlled 'zakat' committees and charitable societies in the West Bank and Gaza. Zakat is an Arabic word referring to the religious obligation to give alms (1). The Koran requires that a portion of zakat be spent on jihad:

- "As-Sadaqat (here it means Zakat) are only for the Fuqara' (poor), and Al-Masakin (the poor) and those employed to collect (the funds); and for to attract the hearts of those who have been inclined (towards Islam); and to free the captives; and for those in debt; **and for Allah's Cause (i.e. for Mujahidun - those fighting in the holy wars)**, and for the wayfarer (a traveller who is cut off from everything); a duty imposed by Allah. And Allah is All-Knower, All-Wise." (Koran 9:60)

The trial investigation began in 2004 when a Baltimore County police officer observed a woman in Islamic dress videotaping support structures of the Chesapeake Bay Bridge and pulled over their vehicle. The driver, Ismail Elbarasse, was detained on an outstanding warrant as a Material Witness to a Hamas case in Chicago and linked to the Hamas leader. In a subsequent search of his home, in a concealed sub-basement, the Federal Bureau of Investigation (FBI) discovered the archives of the Muslim Brotherhood in North America including documents, financial records, videos, audio tapes, photographs and numerous other items (2).

These documents made clear the group's primary objective: to implement Sharia law in America and re-establish a global Caliphate. Most notably, evidence was provided revealing a written strategic plan, led by the Muslim Brotherhood to overthrow the US government and replace it with an Islamic one. Specifically, the visionary Muslim Brotherhood memo, "An Explanatory Memorandum On the General Strategic Goal for the Group In North America.", which reads in part (3):

- '**Four: The Process of Settlement**: In order for Islam and its Movement to become "a part of the homeland" in which it lives, "stable" in its land, "rooted" in the spirits and minds of its people, "enabled" in the live of its society and has firmly-established "organizations" on which the Islamic structure is built and with which the testimony of civilization is achieved, the Movement must plan and struggle to obtain "the keys" and the tools of this process in [sic] carry out this grand mission as a "Civilization Jihadist" responsibility which lies on the shoulders of Muslims and - on top of them - the Muslim Brotherhood in this country.'

- '4. **Understanding the Role of the Muslim Brotherhood in North America**: The process of settlement is a 'Civilization-Jihadist process' with all the word means. The Ikhwan must understand that their work in America is a kind of grand Jihad in eliminating and destroying the Western civilization from within and 'sabotaging' its miserable house by their hands and the hands of the believers so that it is eliminated and God's religion is made victorious over all other religions. Without this level of understanding, we are not up to this challenge and have not prepared ourselves for Jihad yet. It is a Muslim's destiny to perform Jihad and work wherever he is and wherever he lands until the final hour comes, and there is no escape from that destiny except for those who chose to slack...' [U.S. v. Holy Land Foundation, et al., Government Exhibit Elbarasse Search 3, (N.D. Texas 2008).

The last page of 'An Explanatory Memorandum' provides a list of organizations working in the Muslim Brotherhood's Islamic Movement in North America. Many of the organizations are still in existence today and indeed have only expanded their reach. They include:

- Muslim Students Association (MSA)

- Islamic Society of North America (ISNA)

- North American Islamic Trust (NAIT) which is the 'bank' for the Muslim Brotherhood in America

- Fiqh Council of North America (FCNA), formerly the ISNA Fiqh Committee, acting as the Majlis al Shura for the Brotherhood in North America

- Islamic Circle of North America (ICNA)

- Islamic Association of Palestine (IAP) whose leaders now run the Council on American Islamic Relations (CAIR)

- International Institute for Islamic Thought (IIIT)

Also found among the archives was a detailed 'Concept of Operations' outlining a 5-Phase Plan to execute the activities of the Muslim Brotherhood in the U.S. (4):

1. Phase One: Phase of discreet and secret establishment of elite leadership.

2. Phase Two: Phase of gradual appearance on the public scene...establishing a shadow government.

3. Phase Three: Escalation phase, prior to conflict and confrontation with the rulers.

4. Phase Four: Open public confrontation with the Government through exercising the political pressure approach... Training on the use of weapons domestically and overseas in anticipation of zero hour. It has noticeable activities in this regard.

5. Phase Five: Seizing power to establish Islamic Nation

In addition, the 'Implementation Manual (1991-1992) listed the goals to be accomplished by each Department or Committee ensuring the success of their Strategy for the U.S. including: Executive Office, Education, Organizations, The Sisters, The Youth, The Political, Local Work, Youth Organizations, Financial, Social, Matrimonial, The Dawa [conveying the message of Islam to non-Muslims], South America, Security, The Palestine Committee, The Center and Secretariat, Foreign Affairs, Mercy Foundation [i.e. fund collection and distribution] (5).

The 'Council for American Islamic Relations' (CAIR) was also named as an unindicted co-conspirator in the trial (6).

The HLF trial demonstrated that the Islamic Association of Palestine (IAP) played a central role in the Muslim Brotherhood's Palestine Committee. When the Muslim Brotherhood in Gaza established Hamas in 1987, the IAP became its mouthpiece in North America just as CAIR is today (7). Found in the raid was a document entitled 'Important Phone and fax numbers (Palestine Section/America)' which included the names of not only Palestine Committee Members (Hamas) in the U.S. but also the names of 'Nihad Awad' and 'Omar Yehya' aka Omar Ahmad (Founders/Leaders of CAIR) (8). In a 2003 civil deposition Former IAP president and CAIR cofounder Rafeeq Jaber acknowledged IAP's contract with the HLF required them to "promote the HLF in every way we can' (9).

CAIR's Executive Director Nihad Awad initially denied receiving any money from HLF, but after a copy of HLF's five thousand dollar check was produced at the hearing, in a supplemental hearing Awad was forced to acknowledge having received the money (10). When the U.S. government shuttered the Holy Land Foundation in late 2001, CAIR characterized this move as "unjust" and "disturbing" (11). In 2008 the FBI cut off all ties with CAIR owing to their ties with Hamas revealed during the trial (12). As made clear by the Hamas charter itself, Hamas is part of the Muslim Brotherhood (13).

The organization that began with the vision of Hassan al-Banna and leaders such as Sayyid Qutb decades ago is a fact today and a very real one (14).

Sources:

1. 'U.S. Dept of Justice Press Release' May 27, 2009.
https://www.justice.gov/opa/pr/federal-judge-hands-downs-sentences-holy-land-foundation-case

2. 'Raising a Jihadi Generation: Understanding the Muslim Brotherhood Movement in America' John Guandolo (2013) A Handbook for Law Enforcement, Intelligence and Military Professionals p.16

3. 'An Explanatory Memorandum: from the Archives of the Muslim Brotherhood in America' Gov't Exhibit 003-0085 U.S. vs Holy Land Foundation et al.
https://www.centerforsecuritypolicy.org/2013/05/25/an-explanatory-memorandum-from-the-archives-of-the-muslim-brotherhood-in-america/

4. 'Raising a Jihadi Generation: Understanding the Muslim Brotherhood Movement in America' John Guandolo (2013) A Handbook for Law Enforcement, Intelligence and Military Professionals p.17-18

5. 'Raising a Jihadi Generation: Understanding the Muslim Brotherhood Movement in America' John Guandolo (2013) A Handbook for Law Enforcement, Intelligence and Military Professionals p.27-29

6. U.S. Dept of Justice Executive Summary Review of FBI Interactions with the Council on American U.S. Relations (2013) p.1
https://oig.justice.gov/reports/2013/e0707r-summary.pdf?trk=public_post _comment-text

7. Peter Baker, "Whitehouse Disavows U.S. Islamic Group After Leader's Oct 7 Remarks" New York Times, December 8, 2023
https://www.nytimes.com/2023/12/08/us/politics/white-house-cair-nihad -awad.html

8. 'Raising a Jihadi Generation: Understanding the Muslim Brotherhood Movement in America' John Guandolo (2013) A Handbook for Law Enforcement, Intelligence and Military Professionals p. 34

9. Emerson 'Part 1: CAIR Exposed'
http://www.steveemerson.com/2008/03/cair-exposed-part-1---as-iap

10. 'CAIR Exposed Part 2: CAIR's Funding', Investigative Report on Terrorism. March 25, 2008.
https://www.investigativeproject.org/documents/110-cair-exposed-part-2-cair-funding.pdf

11. "CAIR: Islamists Fooling the Establishment," Middle East Quarterly 13, no.2 (Spring 2006),
http://www.meforum.org/916/cair-islamists-fooling-the-establishment

12. Joseph Abrams, "FBI Cuts Ties With CAIR Following Terror Financing Trial" January 30, 2009
https://www.foxnews.com/politics/fbi-cuts-ties-with-cair-following-terror-financing-trial

13. Section Two of the charter begins with the line: The Islamic Resistance Movement is a branch of the Muslim Brotherhood chapter in Palestine. The Hamas Charter can be seen at
https://israeled.org/resources/documents/hamas-charter-islamic-resistance-movement-palestine/

14. Qutb, Sayyid 'Milestones' 1964
https://ia600903.us.archive.org/0/items/MILESTONES_201903/MILESTONES.pdf

CHAPTER THIRTY-THREE

MYTH BUSTER: DID ISLAM IMPROVE THE LIVES OF WOMEN?

T his story begins in Mecca prior to Mohammed's migration to Medina and the beginning of the Islamic calendar. For the first 25 years of his married life Mohammed had only one wife, Khadija. She had hired him to drive her caravans. Khadija was a rich successful widow and sought by many for her wealth (1).

Mohammed did a good job of driving her caravans and so she proposed marriage to him.

Fifteen years after their marriage Mohammed started having revelations. Khadija was his first convert and staunch supporter. She, and his uncle Abu Talib acted as his protectors in Mecca because Mohammed's determination that this poly-theistic society should worship only Allah, and acknowledge Mohammed as his prophet, was not well received. It is in this early period of Mecca that Mohammed said he did not approve of female infanticide and this is. of course, a good thing (Koran 81.8-9)

Many Koranic verses, as in the hadith, address personal situations involving Mo-hammed and/or his followers.

There was no question of veiling Khadija, that revelation didn't come till much later, a full five years after the migration to Medina and after some urging by Mohammed's companion Umar. There are many hadith (stories and traditions about Mohammed) that attest to the lack of veiling during the first 18 years of Mohammed's preaching.

- Narrated 'Aisha: (the wife of the Prophet) 'Umar bin Al-Khattab used to say to Allah's Messenger "Let your wives be veiled" But he did not do so. The wives of the Prophet used to go out to answer the call of nature at night only at Al-Manasi.' Once Sauda, the daughter of Zam'a went out and she was a tall woman. 'Umar bin Al-Khattab saw her while he was in a gathering, and said, "I have recognized you, O Sauda!" He ('Umar) said so as he was anxious for some Divine orders regarding the veil (the veiling of women.) So Allah revealed the Verse of veiling.(Al-Hijab; a complete body cover excluding the eyes). (Bukhari 6240)

Mohammed lost both his protectors when Khadija and Abu Talib died in the same year. Mohammed then married Sauda, and his favourite, six year old Aisha. Three years later Mohammed and his followers migrated to Medina. This marks the beginning of the Islamic calendar, a change of tactics and the end of tolerance for 'Jahiliyya' – the pre-Islamic period of ignorance (2).

Mohammed continued having revelations taking more wives, female slaves and sex slaves as described in many hadith (stories and traditions about Mohammed). He consummated his marriage to Aisha when she was nine:

- Narrated 'Aisha: that the Prophet married her when she was six years old and he consummated his marriage when she was nine years old, and then she remained with him for nine years (i.e., till his death). (al-Nasa'i 3257)

According to Ibn Ishaq's biography (Sira) of Mohammed he married 13 women altogether (3). Allah granted him permission to marry as many wives and to have as many slaves 'as his right hand possessed'. 'We have made lawful to you your wives...(captives or slaves)... relatives and other believing women but this is the privilege for you only'.(Koran 33:50) His followers were limited to four wives. and what their 'right hand possessed'.

Before Mohammed, adoption was customary and Mohammed himself had an adopted son by the name of Zayd. Zayd was married to Zaynab and Mohammed had gone to Zayd's house one day and saw Zaynab alone. Later, Zayd said to Mohammed 'perhaps Zaynab has excited your admiration so I will separate myself from her, so I will divorce her, so you can have her' (4).

Such a thing wasn't customary because Zayd was considered to be Mohammed's son – but then Mohammed had a revelation from Allah about 'Adopted Sons', they are not 'True Sons':

- "Allah has not made for a man two hearts in his interior. And He has not made your wives whom you declare unlawful your mothers. And he has not made your adopted sons your [true] sons. That is [merely] your saying by your mouths, but Allah says the truth, and He guides to the [right] way." (Koran 33:4)

- "And [remember, O Muhammad], when you said to the one on whom Allah bestowed favor and you bestowed favor, "Keep your wife and fear Allah ," while you concealed within yourself that which Allah is to disclose. And you feared the people, while Allah has more right that you fear Him. So when Zayd had no longer any need for her, We married her to you in order that there not be upon the believers any discomfort concerning the wives of their adopted sons when they no longer have need of them. And ever is the command of Allah accomplished." (Koran 33:37)

Because of the revelation, Zayd divorced his wife and Mohammed married her. Since that time, adoption is considered unlawful in Islam.

Before Islam there were singing girls who danced and mocked Mohammed in Mecca, but when Mohammed went back to Mecca 10 years later he ordered them killed (5). Musical instruments were also forbidden. From a handbook of sharia:

- "Allah ordered me to do away with musical instruments flutes strings crucifixes and the affair of the 'pre-Islamic period of ignorance'" (6).

Before Islam women did not have to cover themselves or perform obligatory prayers but after Islam women were instructed to cover themselves, obey and perform obligatory prayers:

- "And abide in your houses and do not display yourselves as [was] the display of the former times of ignorance. And establish prayer and give zakah and obey Allah and His Messenger. Allah intends only to remove from you the impurity [of sin]..." (Koran 33:33)

Veiling was also required to distinguish Muslim women from the unbelievers and captives – they would thereby 'be known and not molested' (Koran 33:59). Reinforcing this requirement Mohammed said that 'Allah does not accept the prayer of a woman who has reached puberty unless she wears a veil' (Dawud 2:641).

Before Islam Mecca was a polytheistic Society with many gods. In fact there were 360 different idols in the Kaaba, but after Islam anyone deliberately missing a prayer should be killed – specifically, a prayer to Allah (7).

- Mohammed said 'oh women give alms as I have seen that the majority of the Dwellers of Hellfire were you women I have not seen anyone more deficient in intelligence than you he said. is not the evidence of two women equal to the witness of one man? this is the deficiency in their intelligence?' (Bukhari 304)

After Islam females became less valued than men in perpetuity owing to Sharia law which cannot be changed. The indemnity for the death or injury of a woman is one half that of a man, the testimony of one man is equal to those of two women. Regarding inheritance, a wife is entitled to only one quarter of a husband's estate where there is no child, or one eighth of the estate where there is a child, and if there is more than one wife this one share will be divided between all the wives together (8).

As for desirable characteristics in a bride, it's recommended for a man to marry a virgin who is fertile but after Islam - religion takes precedence (9).

For her entire life, a woman must have a male guardian and there is a prescribed order of lawful guardianship amongst the bride's relatives to decide in regards to her marriage. Guardians who may marry a virgin to a man without her consent include the bride's father or grandfather. It is recommended to ask her permission if she has reached puberty, which clearly means that she can be married before reaching puberty. A virgin's silence is considered as permission (10).

- Mohammed said "A previously-married woman should not be married until she is consulted, and a virgin should not be married until her consent is sought, and her consent is her silence." (Ibn Majah 1871)

Prepubescent girls can be married owing to Mohammed's example in marrying Aisha when she was only six. Aisha said:

- "I used to play with dolls when I was with the Messenger of Allah, and he used to bring my friends to me to play with me." (Ibn Majah 1982)

In 2022, Iran registered 172 marriages of young girls between the ages of five and nine (11).

A man may divorce his wife by clearly announcing that he repudiates her. a woman can only affect a divorce if she has permission from her husband (12).

The Koran states that men are in charge of women by right of what they spend from their wealth:

- '...so righteous women are devoutly obedient and from those wives from whom you fear arrogance that you should warn them forsake them in bed and finally strike them.' (Koran 4:34)

Which is quite a turn of events because it was Mohammed's first, and only wife for twenty-five years – Khadija who was initially the wealthy partner and offered marriage to him. Revelations authorizing unlimited wives to Mohammed and as many as four to his male followers never occurred until after she had died.

In summary then, before Islam there was Khadija, a rich successful business-woman who not only hired Mohammed to drive her caravans, she proposed marriage to him. There were dancing and singing girls who mocked Mohammed; adoptions were customary there were no veils; no death for deliberately missing prayers and no Sharia.

Today, Sharia permits beating women, limits their legal rights to divorce, inde-pendent agency, inheritance, testimony and more. This is the law, the sharia, the ordained way of Islam. Wherever Sharia is followed closely, whether in a country or in a home, the situation for the woman has not changed in 14 centuries.

The Koran is considered perfect and Mohammed's example is the pattern to follow:

- "Indeed in the Messenger of Allah (Muhammad SAW) you have a good example to follow for him who hopes in (the Meeting with) Allah and the Last Day and remembers Allah much." Koran 33:21

No change is possible after Islam. Is this an improvement? You decide.

Sources:

(1) Guillaume, Alfred. 'The Life of Muhammad: a Translation of Ishaq's Sirat Rasul Allah' (#120) Oxford University Press, 1967 https://archive.org/details/GuillaumeATheLifeOfMuhammad/page/n3/mode/2up

(2) Ibid: (p.219 #324)

(3) Ibid: (p.792 #918)

(4) Al-Tabari Volume VIII p.2 [1461] The Victory of Islam (9thC)

(5) Guillaume, Alfred. 'The Life of Muhammad: a Translation of Ishaq's Sirat Rasul Allah' (#818-821) Oxford University Press, 1967
https://archive.org/details/GuillaumeATheLifeOfMuhammad/page/n3/mode/2up

(6) Reliance of the Traveller Nuh Ha Mim Keller, Amana Publications 2015 (r40.1)
https://archive.org/details/relianceofthetravellertheclassicmanualofislamicsacredlaw

(7) ibid w18:10

(8) Ibid o4.9; o24.7; L6.4

(9) Ibid m3.7

(10) Ibid m3:13; m8:2

(11) NCRI Women Committee 'Iran Registers 172 marriages of young girls between 5 and 9 years old'.
https://women.ncr-iran.org/2022/01/17/172-marriages-of-young-girls/

(12) Reliance of the Traveller Nuh Ha Mim Keller, Amana Publications 2015 (n1.0; n1:1)
https://archive.org/details/relianceofthetravellertheclassicmanualofislamicsacredlaw

RELEVANT DOCTRINE:

Koran 33:21 https://legacy.quran.com/33/21

Koran 33:33 https://legacy.quran.com/33/33

Koran 33:4 https://legacy.quran.com/33/4

Koran 33:37 https://legacy.quran.com/33/37

Koran 33:59 https://legacy.quran.com/33/59

Koran 4:34 https://legacy.quran.com/4/34

Hadith (Bukhari 5133) https://sunnah.com/bukhari:5133

Hadith (Bukhari 6240) https://sunnah.com/bukhari:6240

Hadith (Nasa'i 3257) https://sunnah.com/nasai:3257

Hadith (Ibn Majah 1871) https://sunnah.com/ibnmajah:1871

Hadith (Ibn Majah 1982) https://sunnah.com/ibnmajah:1982

CHAPTER THIRTY-FOUR

WHAT IS DAWA?

D o your deeply held values and beliefs change simply because you've relocated? Likely not. You simply abide by the local laws and all is well.

Many cultures are largely compatible: Thai food for lunch, sharing a seder dinner with a neighbour, a community Easter egg hunt, a folk fest at city hall, a dance at the Edelweiss club, Chinese New Year celebrations or a native art show. Everyone welcome. However, it's unrealistic to believe that the same is true of deeply held values and beliefs, especially when the two are inextricably linked as law.

Case in point, eleven hundred people demonstrating in the streets of Hamburg demanding that an Islamic Caliphate be established (1).

Now a caliphate means sharia which is the Islamic system of law and religion in one. Sharia divides the world into believers (the ummah) vs everybody else. More than half the Koran is about the unbeliever and it's not good news:

- "Indeed, they who disbelieved among the People of the Scripture and the polytheists will be in the fire of Hell, abiding eternally therein. Those are the worst of creatures." (Koran 98:6)

So 'Najasun' (unclean) they are considered too impure to enter the city of Mecca:

- "O you who believe (in Allah's Oneness and in His Messenger)! Verily, the Mushrikun (polytheists, pagans, idolaters, disbelievers ... are Najasun (impure). So let them not come near Al-Masjid-al-Haram (at Makkah) after this year..." (Koran 9:28)

Demands for a Caliphate in Germany; underground 'radical' mosques in Italy (2), Hamas supporters burning cars in Portland, Oregon (3), and increasing jihadi violence (4) are not to be taken lightly, yet their significance and the threat such examples pose to all those who do not follow sharia is excused, forgotten in tomorrow's news – that's if it even makes the news. Why is that?

DAWA

Dawa is the Islamic practice of attempting to convert others to Islam but it is much more than that:

> "Islamist groups have enjoyed not just protection but at times official sponsorship from government agencies duped into regarding them as representatives of "moderate Muslims" simply because they do not engage in violence" (5).
>
> Ali, Ayaan HIrsi 2017

Dawa can be used as a method of stealth jihad and is mentioned fifteen times in the Muslim Brotherhood's 'Explanatory Memorandum' (6).

Many people, especially perceived 'influencers', have been invited to 'Dawa' or 'dialogue events' – sometimes referred to as 'A Common Word'. Pocket Dawa Manuals (7) instruct proponents how to present Islam as a 'religion of peace', and living in a non-Islamic country where they don't have to deal with the reality of sharia, some may be fully convinced that this is so.

Because Islamic doctrine is dualistic in both its attitude towards non-Muslims vs Muslims, and Meccan vs Medinan (jihad) verses, it isn't difficult to select phrases that paint a rosy, albeit very limited picture of Islam. The life of Mohammed belies this rosy picture but his jihad after migrating to Medina, or jihad today, will not be spoken of at these events (8)(9)(10).

This is not unlike the 'good cop, bad cop' scenario.

- Mohammed! "Urge the believers to fight. If there are twenty steadfast persons amongst you, they will overcome two hundred, and if there be a hundred steadfast persons they will overcome a thousand of those who disbelieve, because they (the disbelievers) are people who do not understand." (Koran 8:65)

The hadith is correct, the disbelievers do not understand, and while one 'cop' is an obvious threat (jihad), Dawa is just the opposite. Dawa very effectively conflates people, with doctrine. Participants are sure to leave with an excellent impression and 'immunized' against facts that may differ.

Dawa is a panacea for all things Islam. There is much to see here, don't be fooled.

Sources:

EDUCATIONAL VIDEO: Deception
https://www.youtube.com/watch?v=9eP8tnQEWf8

(1) Germany:
https://www.rt.com/news/596703-islamists-rally-german-caliphate-hamburg/

(2) U.S. News:
https://www.breitbart.com/local/2024/05/07/oregon-pro-palestinian-group-takes-responsibility-for-setting-police-cars-on-fire/

(3) Italy:
https://www.rt.com/news/596285-italy-rome-mosques-concerns/

(4) April attacks:

https://thereligionofpeace.com/attacks/attacks.aspx?Yr=Last30

(5) Ali, Ayaan HIrsi "The Challenge of Dawa Political Islam as Ideology and Movement and How to Counter It" (p.3) Hoover Institution Press, Stanford University 2017

(6) Muslim Brotherhood Explanatory Memorandum:

https://centerforsecuritypolicy.org/wp-content/uploads/2013/04/CSP-Explanatory-Memorandum.pdf

(7) Pocket Dawa Manual

https://www.muslim-library.com/dl/books/English_Pocket_Dawah_Manual.pdf

(8) Guillaume, Alfred. 'The Life of Muhammad: a Translation of Ishaq's Sirat Rasul Allah' Oxford University Press, 1967

https://archive.org/details/GuillaumeATheLifeOfMuhammad/page/n3/mode/2up

(8) Attacks last 30 days:

https://thereligionofpeace.com/attacks/attacks.aspx?Yr=Last30

(10) Reliance of the Traveller (o9:14) Nuh Ha Mim Keller, Amana Publications 2015 (ROT)

https://archive.org/details/relianceofthetravellertheclassicmanualofislamicsacredlaw

RELEVANT DOCTRINE:

Koran 3:28 https://legacy.quran.com/3/28

Koran 8:65 https://legacy.quran.com/8/65

Koran 9:1 https://legacy.quran.com/9/1

Koran 9:29 https://legacy.quran.com/9/29

Koran 13:41 https://legacy.quran.com/13/41

Koran 48:29 https://legacy.quran.com/48/29

Koran 66:2 https://legacy.quran.com/66/2

Hadith (Muslim 2889a) https://sunnah.com/muslim:2889a

Hadith (Bukhari 3167 https://sunnah.com/bukhari:3167

Hadith (Bukhari 3941) https://sunnah.com/bukhari:3941

Hadith (Muslim 2793) https://sunnah.com/muslim:2793

Hadith (ibn Majah 225) https://sunnah.com/ibnmajah:225

Hadith (Bukhari 3030) https://sunnah.com/bukhari:3030

Hadith (Bukhari 3053) https://sunnah.com/bukhari:3053

CHAPTER THIRTY-FIVE

SHOOTING THE MESSENGER DOESN'T CHANGE THE MESSAGE

So Sheikh Kathrada has made the news again (1). This time it's for his sermons against Jews but at Christmas and Easter Christians top the bill (2). During the rest of the year any unbeliever will do.

Sermons such as this are certainly not unique to Canada, the tragedy in silencing the Sheikh is that by addressing the person, rather than the doctrine, the truth matters not (3). The Sheikh's Muslim Youth Group YouTube channel has over 500 videos and almost 2,000 followers for a reason.

It's not that what he's saying about the 'unbeliever' is false or 'radical', you can compare the statements in his sermon to the Islamic doctrine and decide for yourself below. It's just that enough of it is said in English, and regularly broadcast on YouTube, that non-Muslims can also share this information and readily understand some of it. What is said in Arabic, is only exposed on the rare occasion when an organization such as MEMRI TV provides a translation.

It does seem reasonable to ask why organizations such as this that promote Sharia (offering ISLAMIC OR LEGAL marriages) are given charity status and provided with government grants in non-Islamic countries thereby allowing sharia to supercede the law of the land (4)(5)(6). Sharia does not recognize equality before the law or freedom of religion and in this example is contrary to the Canadian Charter of Rights and Freedoms (7)(8).

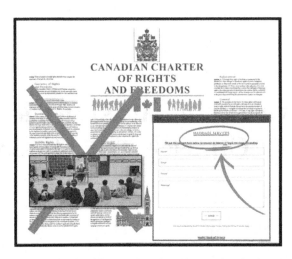

The EU Parliamentary Assembly reports that sharia clearly discriminates against women:

"8. The Assembly is also concerned about the "judicial" activities of "Sharia councils" in the United Kingdom. Although they are not considered part of the British legal system, Sharia councils attempt to provide a form of alternative dispute resolution, whereby members of the Muslim community, sometimes voluntarily, often under considerable social pressure, accept their religious jurisdiction mainly in **marital issues and Islamic divorce proceedings** but also in matters relating to inheritance and Islamic commercial contracts. **The Assembly is concerned that the rulings of the Sharia councils clearly discriminate against women in divorce and inheritance cases. The Assembly is aware that informal Islamic courts may also exist in other Council of Europe member States**" (9).

COMPARISON BETWEEN WORDS OF THE SHEIKH AND VERSES FROM THE KORAN: (timing corresponds to the video)

SHEIKH KATHRADA:

SK 0:04 Non-Muslims are the enemy of Allah, therefore they are your enemies

KORAN 8:59 And **let not those who disbelieve think they will escape**. Indeed, they will not cause failure [to Allah].

KORAN 8:60 "Against them make ready your strength to the utmost of your power, including steeds of war, to **strike terror into (the hearts of) the enemies of Allah and your enemies,** and others besides, whom ye may not know, but whom Allah doth know. Whatever ye shall spend in the cause of Allah, shall be repaid unto you, and ye shall not be treated unjustly.

SK 1:11 'You think that they are your friends? No, they're the enemies of Allah.

KORAN 3:28 **Believers should not take unbelievers as friends** in preference to other believers. **Those who do this will have none of Allah's protection** and will only have themselves as guards. Allah warns you to fear Him for all will return to Him.

SK 1:22 'Friends, I want our children to understand this, the non-Muslims are the enemies of Allah – therefore they are your enemies. Some of them don't even believe Allah exists. You want somebody like that to be a close friend of yours?' Enough is enough.

KORAN 3:118 **Believers! Do not become friends with anyone except your own people. The unbelievers will not rest until they have corrupted you.** They wish nothing but your ruin. Their hatred of you is made clear by their words, but even greater hatred is hidden within their hearts. We have made Our signs clear to you. Therefore, do your best to comprehend them.

SK 1:57 the Zionist Jews had horrible predecessors and today they are even worse than their predecessors ...

KORAN 1:6-7 **Guide us to the Straight Way** (7) The Way of those on whom You have bestowed Your Grace , **not (the way) of those who earned Your Anger (such as the Jews), nor of those who went astray (such as the Christians).**

KORAN 4:47 **O you who have been given the Scripture (Jews and Christians)! Believe in what We have revealed (to Muhammad)** confirming what is (already) with you, **before We efface faces** (by making them like the back of necks; without nose, mouth, eyes, etc.) and turn them hindwards, **or curse them as We cursed the Sabbath-breakers. And the Commandment of Allah is always executed.**

SK 2:15 "They are those whom Allah has cursed and with whom he became angry and he made some of them apes and pigs'

KORAN 5:60 Say (O Muhammad to the people of the Scripture): "**Shall I inform you of something worse than that**, regarding the recompense from Allah: **those (Jews) who incurred the Curse of Allah and His Wrath, those of whom (some) He transformed into monkeys and swines**, those who worshipped Taghut (false deities); such are worse in rank (on the Day of Resurrection in the Hell-fire), and far more astray from the Right Path (in the life of this world)."

SK 3:42 'Zionists are occupiers, they are the aggressors, they came to a land that doesn't belong to them

KORAN 60:1 O you who believe! **Take not My enemies and your enemies (i.e. disbelievers** and polytheists, etc.) **as friends, showing affection towards them**, while **they have disbelieved** in what has come to you of the truth (i.e. Islamic Monotheism, this Quran, and Muhammad SAW), **and have driven out the Messenger (Muhammad SAW) and yourselves (from your homeland) because you believe in Allah your Lord!** If you have come forth to strive in My Cause and to seek My Good Pleasure, (then **take not these disbelievers and polytheists, etc., as your friends**). You show friendship to them in secret, while I am All-Aware of what you conceal and what you reveal. And whosoever of you (Muslims) does that, then indeed he has gone (far) astray, (away) from the Straight Path.

SK 4:13 ' Oh Allah, bring annihilation upon the plundering and criminal Jews.. show us the black day that you inflict upon them, make their plots backfire on them. Oh Allah shake the ground under their feet.

KORAN 3:54 **And they (the disbelievers) schemed, and Allah schemed (against them): and Allah is the best of schemers**

SK 11:52 'What does Allah say in the Koran about himself? He begets not nor is he begotten. He doesn't have children and He is not the child of anyone' How are they not the enemies of Allah?'

KORAN 19:35 **It befits not (the Majesty of) Allah that He should beget a son [this refers to the slander of Christians against Allah,** by saying that 'Iesa (Jesus) is the son of Allah]. Glorified (and Exalted be He above all that they associate with Him). When He decrees a thing, He only says to it, "Be!" and it is.

SK 12:26 'How are they not the enemies of Allah, when they accuse Allah of being tight-fisted, of being stingy, of not being generous.

KORAN 4:37 **Those who are miserly** and enjoin miserliness on other men **and hide what Allah has bestowed upon them of His Bounties. And We have prepared for the disbelievers a disgraceful torment.**

SK 12:37 'You know when the Jews said that, Allah responded to them by saying 'Let their hands be shackled'. May they be tight-fisted, may their hands be tied.

KORAN 5:64 "The Jews say: "Allah's hand is tied up." **Be their hands tied up and be they accursed for the (blasphemy) they utter.** Nay, both **His hands are widely outstretched: He giveth and spendeth (of His bounty) as He pleaseth..."**

Some people like to imagine that Islamic doctrine can be reformed – they may even declare 'that's not my Islam' but would never dare to say this out loud in an Islamic state. There is now good reason to hesitate even in Canada (10).

After Mohammed's Migration to Medina, marking the beginning of the Islamic calendar in 622 CE, fully 17% of the Koran and 9% of the Hadith contain anti-Jew text (11). Within five years all the Jews in Medina had either been exiled or killed (12).

It is folly to think that in 14 centuries there have not been others who wanted Islam to be something that it is not. They may be useful for a time, just like the poorly informed (13) Gays for Gaza (so long as they stay on their own side of the street)(14). But abandoned, at best, when the rally is over (15).

SOURCES:

(1) Sheikh re Jews 2024:
https://www.youtube.com/watch?v=ULpa-8OHZVo&t=632s

(2) Sheikh re Christians Dec. 2021:
https://www.memri.org/reports/canadian-imam-younus-kathrada-congratulating-people-christmas-congratulating-murderers-and

(3) Solomon, S & Alamaqdisi, E. 'The Mosque Exposed' ANM Press 2007

(4) Muslim Youth Group YouTube Channel: https://www.youtube.com/@MuslimYouthVictoria

(5) Dar ul-Ihsan Islamic Centre for Islamic Education and Muslim School Charity registration:
https://apps.cra-arc.gc.ca/ebci/hacc/srch/pub/t3010/v26/t3010ovrvw

(6) Hussain, Ed 'Among the Mosques, Journey across Muslim Britain' (p. 252-53) Bloomsbury (2021)

(7)Youth Group given city grant:
https://globalnews.ca/news/10294929/antisemitism-canada-since-oct-7/

(8) Canadian Charter of Rights and Freedoms:
https://www.canada.ca/content/dam/pch/documents/services/download-order
-charter-bill/canadian-charter-rights-freedoms-eng.pdf

(9) EU Parliamentary Assembly #8:
https://assembly.coe.int/nw/xml/XRef/Xref-XML2HTML-en.asp?fileid=253
53

(10) Pro-Hamas leaders in Canada:
https://www.bitchute.com/video/Bpe-UgfrkUM/

(11) Statistical Analysis:
https://www.cspii.org/learn-political-islam/methodology/statistical-analysis-pol
itical-islam/anti-jew-text-trilogy/

(12) Charter of Medina:
https://perspectivesonislam.substack.com/p/is-the-charter-of-medina-significa
nt

(13) LGBTQ+ video:
https://x.com/OliLondonTV/status/1797982520417595704

(14) News: Pride Parade blocked
https://torontosun.com/news/world/trouble-in-paradise-pro-palestine-protest
ers-block-philly-gay-pride-parade

(15) News Video 9:50 min:
https://www.youtube.com/watch?v=ULpa-8OHZVo&t=632s

RELEVANT DOCTRINE:

Koran 8:59-60 https://legacy.quran.com/8/59-60

Koran 3:28 https://legacy.quran.com/3/28

Koran 3:118 https://legacy.quran.com/3:118

Koran 1:6-7 https://legacy.quran.com/1/6-7

Koran 4:47 https://legacy.quran.com/4/47

Koran 5:60 https://legacy.quran.com/5/60

Koran 60:1 https://legacy.quran.com/60:1

Koran 3:54 https://legacy.quran.com/3/54

Koran 19:35 https://legacy.quran.com/19/35

Koran 4:37 https://legacy.quran.com/4/37

Koran 5:64 https://legacy.quran.com/5/64

CHAPTER THIRTY-SIX

DERADICALIZATION PROGRAMMES

Do they make any sense?

Police in Perth, Australia recently shot and killed a teen who had stabbed a random stranger in a car park. Newspaper reports read 'There are indications he had been radicalized online' after 'converting to Islam'. He was said to have 'mental health issues' but was also undergoing a 'police deradicalization course' (1).

In another case, an Afghan national who repeatedly publicly exposed himself was found guilty, but on appeal was not deported because a doctor claimed that if he did this in Afghanistan he could be the victim of mob violence because of 'mental health issues'. This is the third time a court decision against him has been reversed by an Asylum Tribunal. He is now free to continue breaching public decency in the U.K (2).

Also in 2024, it made headlines around the globe when, in the middle of a church service, an internationally known Bishop was stabbed multiple times right in front of his congregation. Parishioners, many of whom are Assyrian Christians who had already fled conflicts in the Middle East, were able to catch and restrain the youth 'who had recently been radicalized' until police arrived. Several more youth were picked up shortly thereafter (3).

Is this really that surprising when a recent survey conducted by the Criminological Research Institute of Lower Saxon found that half of young German Muslims want sharia in Germany and almost 70% said that the rules of the Koran are more important than the law of the country. In Hamburg recently thousands marched through the streets demanding an Islamic caliphate (4)(5).

So which is it? What is 'radical' and how much of a difference is there between that and 'mental health issues' or is it really just a matter of perspective.

Does it actually make sense to determine the state of a person's mental health based on the norms of the host community rather than the norms of sharia if the perpetrator is Muslim? If behaviour is perfectly acceptable according to sharia, but happens to be practiced in a non-Islamic country – that is not a mental health issue, it is a legal one. Sharia vs the law of the land but this is what isn't addressed or even discussed.

One reason for this is that authorities in non-Islamic countries discount 'religion' as a motivation. In a 2022 report prepared by the Australian Institute of Criminology for the 'Countering Violent Extremism Branch, Dept. of Home Affairs,' we read: ***of the few studies that have examined religion OTHER than Islam**, including Judaism, Christianity and Hinduism, results did not support a connection to a terrorism outcome (Desmarais et al. 2017). Ultimately, **religious affiliation does not appear to be a meaningful or widely applicable risk factor for violent extremism*** (6).

This same study describes 'jihadism' as an 'extremist ideology' ergo a mental health issue when in fact, jihad is normative Islamic doctrine. And even though instructors may laud the advice of Sun Tsu to 'know the enemy and yourself', students of counter-terrorism will find little mention of Islamic doctrine or the authentic life of Mohammed in their study materials (7)(8). Are not knife wielding jihadis the enemy? Instead, using tools provided in the deradicalization program what they will discover are programmes "developed in consultation with

Imams and Muslim community leaders" or 'faith leaders' (9)(10). But what does the Islamic faith teach?

- Mohammed said, "The person who participates in (Holy battles) in Allah's cause and nothing compels him to do so except belief in Allah and His Apostles, will be recompensed by Allah either with a reward, or booty (if he survives) or will be admitted to Paradise (if he is killed in the battle as a martyr). Had I not found it difficult for my followers, then I would not remain behind any sariya going for Jihad and I would have loved to be martyred in Allah's cause and then made alive, and then martyred and then made alive, and then again martyred in His cause.'" (Bukhari 36)

Mohammed is the guiding light of Islam, it is his example that adherents are required to follow. 'He who obeys the messenger [Mohammed] has indeed obeyed Allah...' (Koran 4:80) A variation on this theme is repeated frequently throughout the Koran and Hadith.

How do the authorities in non-Islamic countries square that circle when it comes to jihad? Does it make sense that this is called 'extremist' when the foundational doctrine of Islam frequently cites jihad in the 'cause of Allah' as the best deed and that Mohammed's behaviour is not that of a 'madman' (Koran 68:2) but indeed, that of 'great moral character' (Koran 68:4).

While police send youth to 'deradicalization' courses government ministers cite the need for "youth programmes addressing health, social services and education" (11)(12). Deradicalization programme directors suggest these are social failures causing economic insecurity and alienation resulting in mental health issues (13). Youth are sometimes in these programmes for years while at the same time trying to convert others to Islam (14)(15).

Now what do course leaders tell the youth – don't follow that part of your doctrine or that example of Mohammed? Of course they don't. Instead Islamic 'religious leaders' are called on for advice. But consider that this is their belief system as well and it is forbidden to be critical of Mohammed. '...whoever conceals (the faults of) a Muslim, Allah will conceal him (his faults) in this world and the Day of Resurrection" (Ibn Majah 225).

So how successful can de-radicalization programmes be? Non-Muslim programme leaders don't study the doctrine for themselves to learn about the dualistic nature of both the doctrine and its attitude towards the non-Muslim. They seem to be unaware that sharia calls for jihad against the non-Muslim and that is exactly what the perpetrators have done (16). From an Islamic perspective, how is that bad?

In some parts of the world killing an unbeliever will hardly raise an eyebrow (17). Perhaps it's time to take Sun Tsu's advice to heart and learn what the doctrine actually teaches about jihad and the unbeliever before expecting that its followers will ignore it.

Sources:

(1) Australia News:
https://www.rt.com/news/597010-radical-stabbing-attack-australia/

(2) UK News:
https://www.thepublica.com/uk-asylum-tribunal-rules-that-migrant-sex-offender-cant-be-deported-because-afghanistan-stigmatizes-sex-offenders/

(3) Australia News:
https://www.rt.com/news/596522-australia-terrorism-police-raid/

(4) Germany News:
https://www.breitbart.com/europe/2024/04/22/germany-nearly-half-of-young

early-half-of-young-muslims-want-islamic-theocracy-third-understand-vio-lent-retribution-for-insulting-mohammed/

(5) New York Post:
https://nypost.com/2024/04/29/world-news/protesters-call-for-islamic-sta
te-in-germany-caliphate-is-the-solution/

(6) AIC report:
https://www.aic.gov.au/sites/default/files/2023-05/sr14.pdf

(7) Guillaume, Alfred. 'The Life of Muhammad: a Translation of Ishaq's
Sirat Rasul Allah', Oxford University Press, 1967 (Ibn Ishaq 700-767CE)
https://archive.org/details/history-ibn-ishaq-sirat-rasul-allah-the-life-of-mu
hammad/page/n7/mode/2up

(8) Counter-terrorism course material:
https://www.vera-2r.nl/

(9) Countering Violent Extremism Evaluation tool:
https://www.cveevaluation.nsw.gov.au/program-finder/being-muslim-bein
g-british

(10) WA Today News:
https://www.watoday.com.au/politics/western-australia/why-didn-t-wa-s-p
rogram-to-counter-violent-extremism-work-20240506-p5fpal.html

(11) Government Summit:
https://minister.homeaffairs.gov.au/ClareONeil/Pages/ministerial-summit
-on-youth-radicalisation.aspx

(12) ABC News: 'Are deradicalization programmes enough?'
https://www.abc.net.au/news/2024-05-06/perth-teenager-shot-police-wille
tton-deradicalisation-program/103807392

(13) Australia 9 News:
https://www.9news.com.au/national/how-do-deradicalisation-programs-work/
da1a9a51-6951-4a4d-a39f-b8d7bbcadcc7

(14) Australia associated press:
https://au.news.yahoo.com/radicalisation-programs-despite-attacks-expert-013
557016.html?guccounter=1

(15) WA Today News:
https://www.watoday.com.au/national/western-australia/final-texts-of-radicalis
ed-perth-schoolboy-revealed-20240506-p5fp4e.html

(16) Jihad (Bukhari Hadith)
https://cspi-web-media.ams3.cdn.digitaloceanspaces.com/documents/Jihad_H
adith-all_-_Copy.pdf

(17) Jihad attacks:
https://thereligionofpeace.com/

RELEVANT DOCTRINE:

Koran 4:80 https://legacy.quran.com/4/80

Koran 45:18 https://legacy.quran.com/45/18

Koran 35:59 https://legacy.quran.com/33/59

Koran 68:2 https://legacy.quran.com/68/2

Koran 68:4 https://legacy.quran.com/68/4

Hadith (Ibn Majah 225) https://sunnah.com/ibnmajah:225

Hadith (Bukhari 36) https://sunnah.com/bukhari:36

Hadith (Nasa'i 2624) https://sunnah.com/nasai:2624

Chapter Thirty-Seven

WHAT'S HAPPENING WITH ISLAMIC INFLUENCE ON WESTERN UNIVERSITIES AND WHY IS IT HAPPENING?

The Fatwa – 1979

I well remember meeting up with a couple fellows in London, England who had been working on the oil rigs in Saudi Arabia in 1980. They quickly became good friends and told the most amazing stories of incredible wealth attained through the recent discovery of oil and the ostentatious spending of it by the Saudi elites. Tables so loaded with food they were groaning with the weight, their luxury chauffeur driven limos riding up and down the streets were apparent in London as well. I remember an evening spent speaking with a Saudi lawyer at the 'Wellington' pub who talked about the many wonderful international business transactions he was involved in, all stemming from the astonishing and sudden wealth coming from the Middle East.

Not everyone was so pleased. In 1979 a coup had occurred at the Grand Mosque in Mecca over this very thing, the liberalization of Islamic norms, corruption by the infidels through media – especially television, and flagrant disregard for sharia promised by the Saudi royal family when they came to power with the help of the reformist Sunni Wahhabis clerics in the 18th century. As is often the case with

Islam, in accordance with the doctrine, the timing was significant – the first day of the new century 1400 in the Islamic calendar (1).

- "Allah will raise for this community at the end of every hundred years the one who will renovate its religion for it." (Dawud 4291)

The coup was not the failure it is made out to be. The perpetrators were demanding the expulsion of non-Muslims (only Muslims can become citizens in Saudi Arabia (2)), a reversal of the secularism that was quickly taking hold in the country, and claimed that they had the 'Mahdi' – an Islamic deliverer that is supposed to appear at the 'end times' (3)(4).

When the police arrived it rained bullets on them but firing a gun within the precincts of the Kaaba is forbidden, if they were killed while shooting would they go to hell? and so the police retreated. A news blackout was employed while Saudi authorities sought help from the 'Ulama' (Islamic scholars and clerics) to find a solution. That solution was a fatwa – a fatwa that would absolve the soldiers of any 'wrong doing' and satisfy those who had heard about the 'Mahdi' – a ruling that was to have far reaching effects for educational institutions across the entire non-Islamic world.

Yes, the coup was short and the perpetrators sentenced to death – but it was not a failure. While the scholars agreed that the 'Mahdi' was not genuine, they sympathized with the intent and demands of the insurgents. They agreed that the Saudis were on the wrong track, that a return to the way of sharia, and a repudiation of secular liberalism must take place. The clerics held the power and they used it (5).

After 3 days of intense discussion the Ulama agreed to support the royal family, but there were conditions – including that Saudi Petro dollars would be spent to spread Islam in the world and allocate billions of dollars towards this programme. An essential detail that was omitted in later news reports (6). With these conditions in place, the scholars signed the fatwa saying that the rebels were wrong and action could be taken against them. Many were killed. A month later, 63 militants were publicly beheaded and the modernization of Saudi Arabia was arrested for decades (7).

But what of the billions?

A look at today's campuses provides the answer as we witness the fruit of this fatwa. Billions from the Saudis and Qatar have poured into the educational system of non-Islamic countries right around the globe and have done so for many years now (8). Already, in 2011 British universities were being described by MPs and Peers as 'hotbeds of Islamic extremism' endangering national security (9). Universities that have been only too happy to accept these windfalls, heedless of the fact that Sharia contravenes the Universal Declaration of Human Rights and the predictable consequences. Ivy league universities in the U.S. have received at least 8 billion in funding from Qatar, Saudi Arabia, the United Emirates and Kuwait (10)(11).

"'If you look at Carnegie Mellon, George Washington University, they actually have campuses in Qatar, and we know that Qatar is a country that's against open and free exchange of ideas and expression. So what is being taught to students on these campuses?" (12)(13).

We don't have to guess, just turn on the news. This is one of the many ways in which formerly non-Islamic countries become Islamic. With Islam comes sharia, no freedom of religion, no equality before the law.

There is a solution. Don't take the money and know the reason why.

Sources:

(1) Trofimov, Yaroslav 'The Siege of Mecca: The 1979 Uprising at Mecca's Holiest Shrine, 2008

(2) The Week:
https://www.theweek.in/news/world/2021/11/12/saudi-arabia-to-grant-ci
tizenship-for-expats-how-does-it-work-who-are-eligible.html

(3) Interview/podcast Trofimov:
https://www.npr.org/2019/11/29/783681014/when-militants-took-mecca
-a-short-siege-with-an-immense-legacy

(4) Der Spiegel:
https://www.spiegel.de/geschichte/anschlag-in-mekka-1979-wie-der-islami
stische-terror-begann-a-1070500.html

(5) Video: When King Khalid Needed a Fatwa:
https://www.youtube.com/watch?v=dTUcdDRpE9Q

(6) BBC News:
https://www.bbc.com/news/stories-50852379

(7) Mosque Seizure:
https://en.wikipedia.org/wiki/Grand_Mosque_seizure

(8) Sewell, Gilbert 'Islam in the Classroom' 2008
https://files.eric.ed.gov/fulltext/ED501724.pdf

(9) Telegraph UK:
https://web.archive.org/web/20111124074133/https://www.telegraph.co.
uk/news/religion/8478975/University-campuses-are-hotbeds-of-Islamic-ex
tremism.html

(10) Fox News:
https://www.foxbusiness.com/media/funding-from-arab-countries-us-univ
ersities-raises-questions-almost-always-come-strings-attached

(11) Qatari Funding:
https://en.wikipedia.org/wiki/Qatari_involvement_in_higher_education_in_t
he_United_States

(12) ABC News:
https://abcstlouis.com/news/nation-world/foreign-countries-send-billions-of-d
ollars-to-top-us-universities-not-a-surprise-were-seeing-anti-israel-protests-on-co
llege-campuses-ivy-league-middle-east-qatar

(13) Hindustan Times:
https://www.hindustantimes.com/world-news/us-news/florida-lawmaker-accu
ses-a-states-muslim-school-of-training-future-terrorists-101715820200583.htm
l

RELEVANT DOCTRINE

Koran 45:18 https://legacy.quran.com/45/18

Koran 9:14 https://legacy.quran.com/9/14

Koran 13:41 https://legacy.quran.com/13/41

Koran 98.6 https://legacy.quran.com/98/6

Hadith (Dawud 4291) https://sunnah.com/abudawud:4291

Hadith (Muslim 22) https://sunnah.com/muslim:22

Hadith (Muslim 2889a) https://sunnah.com/muslim:2889a

Hadith (Ibn Majah 3952) https://sunnah.com/ibnmajah:3952

Hadith (Bukhari 2977) https://quranx.com/Hadith/Bukhari/USC-MSA/Vol
ume-4/Book-52/Hadith-220

Hadith (Nasa'i 5659) https://sunnah.com/nasai:5659

CHAPTER THIRTY-EIGHT

PARADISE FOR WHO?

Listen up true reformers (as opposed to those who only seem to be) – Islamic doctrine is not on your side! Yet another stabbing has occurred in Germany while the perpetrator shouts 'Allahu, Akbar'! (1)

And for what exactly? Mohammed himself was not sure he would be rewarded with 'paradise':

- Koran 46:9 "I am not something original among the messengers, nor do **I know what will be done with me** or with you. I only follow that which is revealed to me, and I am not but a clear warner."

According to the Koran, Allah would cut Mohammed's aorta if he made up false sayings:

- Koran 69:44-46 "And **if Muhammad had made up about Us some false sayings**, We would have seized him by the right hand; Then **We would have cut from him the aorta.**"

So were Mohammed's sayings false? From the Hadith:

- Mohammed "in his ailment in which he died, used to say, "O `Aisha! I still feel the pain caused by the food I ate at Khaibar, and at this time, **I feel as if my aorta is being cut from that poison.**" (Bukhari 4428)

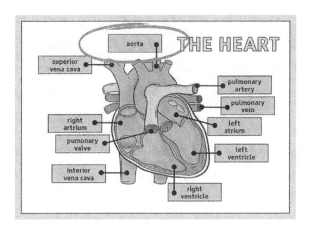

There are many kinds of jihad, and while violent jihad is obvious, stealth jihad – the so-called 'Islamists' – are not, they don't wear a sign and its pure hubris to think they are readily detected even by those who are well versed in the subject. Whether it's on the campus or providing advice to politicians and security services, does it make sense to seek advice from people that may run counter to the requirements of their beliefs? (2) Particularly when statistics indicate that these beliefs are strongly supported by Muslims in non-Islamic countries? (3)

- '...whoever conceals (the faults of) a Muslim, Allah will conceal him (his faults) in this world and the Day of Resurrection" (Ibn Majah 225)

- Let not believers take disbelievers as allies rather than believers. And whoever [of you] does that has nothing with Allah , **except when taking precaution against them in prudence**... (Koran 3:28)

- "Scholars say that **there is no harm in giving a misleading impression if required by an interest countenanced by Sacred Law**..." ('Reliance of the Traveller' r10.3)

How else to explain the numbers? Only 23% of British Muslims surveyed oppose sharia. For many, it's a sense of community, but then again, they aren't living in an Islamic country and for the women at least, they might find it quite a shock if they were. For others seeking power and control, they can rely on the doctrine to provide it (4). Sharia, the ordained way of Islam, includes stoning adulterers, cutting off the hands and feet of thieves, a woman's testimony is worth half that of a man and death to apostates. By Western standards, it is these normative Islamic values that are extreme and yet it is these practices that are upheld by the doctrine.

- (Remember) when your Lord inspired the angels, "Verily, I am with you, so keep firm those who have believed. I will cast terror into the hearts of those who have disbelieved, so strike them over the necks, and smite over all their fingers and toes." (Koran 8:12)

A former colleague of mine used to study in London at a small reformist mosque that boasted a mere 20 members at Friday service while the traditional mosque down the road attracted 800. This is unsurprising as the doctrine demands conformity, not reform, and the doctrine cannot be changed (5).

For example, in 2022, author Salman Rushie was stabbed and almost killed owing to a death fatwa issued by the Ayatollah Khomeini in 1989 (6). His crime? Publishing a novel that was deemed disrespectful towards Islam. A novel that, by non-Islamic standards, pales in comparison to the Ayatollah's own writings, 'Tahrir al-Wasilah' regarding temporary wives (often very young girls), slave-girls and much more (7). Writings that are practiced and taught by other Imams – highly respected Islamic scholars today (8). When it comes to the doctrine, it is the Imams who have the moral high ground, not those seeking reform.

- '...The truest of word is the Book of Allah and best of guidance is the guidance of Muhammad. The worst of things are those that are newly invented; every newly-invented thing is an innovation and every innovation is going astray, and every going astray is in the Fire...'(al-Nasa'i 1578)

It is the rare case that makes headlines but here are just a few:

- 2024 Michael Sturzenberger, former leader of the German Freedom Party was stabbed numerous times in Mannheim as were the policeman and bystanders who tried to intervene (1)

- 2024 U.K. Politician withdraws her candidacy after receiving rape and death threats (9)

- 2024 In Europe, women are similarly afraid to attend events owing to attacks (10)(11)

- 2023 UK Imam described as a 'highly esteemed and exemplary figure' with a 'tireless commitment to promoting Quranic education', also instructs how to stone women properly and was awarded a 2.2 million pound grant to support young people in Birmingham (12)(13)

- 2023 U.K. teacher was given a new identity and is still hiding in fear years after showing students the Charlie Hebdo cartoon of Mohammed (14)

- 2023 France, court case begins. Teacher beheaded for showing Mohammed cartoons even though he had asked Muslim students to leave the room (15)

- 2022 Sir David Amess, a British Conservative Party politician was fatally stabbed at a constituency open-house in Essex. His killer was Ali Harbi Ali, a British Islamic State sympathiser (16)

In summary, according to Islamic doctrine, it's not the 'jihadis' and 'Islamists' that are extreme, but rather those that seek reform. The doctrine is the source, jihad is only the effect.

Sources:

(1) CBS News:
https://www.cbsnews.com/news/germany-knife-stabbing-attack-mannheim-video-anti-islam-activist-michael-sturzenberger/

(2) MSN News:
https://www.msn.com/en-us/news/world/civil-service-guidance-directed-officia
ls-to-website-that-likened-homosexuality-to-a-scourge/ar-BB1k106T

(3) Survey:
https://henryjacksonsociety.org/wp-content/uploads/2024/04/HJS-Deck-200
324-Final.pdf

(4) Ibrahim, Raymond 'The al Qaeda Reader' Boradway Books 2007

(5) Salman Rushdie:
https://en.wikipedia.org/wiki/Stabbing_of_Salman_Rushdie

(6) Khomeini, Imam Rhouhullah, 'Tahrir al-Wasilah' (p.66, 316, 401, 531, 703
+)
http://ijtihadnet.com/wp-content/uploads/3042.pdf

(7) Video: temporary marriage with imam of very young girl
https://www.bitchute.com/video/x0QkYRT0ziQH/

(8) Article:
https://perspectivesonislam.substack.com/p/can-islam-be-modernized

(9) U.K. Politician withdraws
https://www.bbc.com/news/articles/c166r49ee3wo

(10) European women afraid:
https://www.msn.com/en-us/news/world/report-finds-over-7000-women-in-ge
rmany-have-been-sexually-assaulted-by-asylum-seekers-since-2015/ar-AA1mtrg
w

(11) European rapes since 2015
https://www.youtube.com/watch?v=2Q27igsYNNY

(12) UK Imam teaches how to stone women properly:
https://onlinequraninstitute.org/our_team/qari-zakaullah-saleem/

(13) Mosque awarded money to build youth centre:
https://mailonline.pressreader.com/article/282269554970989

(14) UK Teacher in hiding:
https://www.express.co.uk/news/uk/1743624/Teacher-in-hiding-prophet-Mo
hammed-cartoon-Batley-Grammar-School-West-Yorkshire

(15) France:
https://www.aljazeera.com/news/2023/11/27/six-teens-in-court-in-connection
-with-beheading-of-french-teacher

(16) MP David Amess:
https://en.wikipedia.org/wiki/Murder_of_David_Amess

RELEVANT DOCTRINE

Koran 3:28 https://legacy.quran.com/3/28

Koran 8:12 https://legacy.quran.com/8/12

Koran 69: 44-46 https://legacy.quran.com/69/44-46

Koran 46:9 https://legacy.quran.com/46/9

Hadith (Dawud 4291) https://sunnah.com/abudawud:4291

Hadith (Ibn Majah 225) https://sunnah.com/ibnmajah:225

Hadith (Nasa'i 1578) https://sunnah.com/nasai:1578

Hadith (Bukhari 4428) https://sunnah.com/bukhari:4428

Sharia: Reliance of the Traveller (r10.3) Umdat al-Salik trans by Nuh Ha Mim
Keller, Amana Publications 2015
https://archive.org/details/relianceofthetravellertheclassicmanualofislamicsacre
dlaw

CHAPTER THIRTY-NINE

SHARIA IN A NUTSHELL

I NTRODUCTION:

Sharia is something most people know something about but often think that it doesn't affect them because they are not Muslim. What they don't recognize is that more than half the Koran is about the non-Muslim, the 'unbeliever' and like it or not, sharia does affect the non-Muslim, sometimes very significantly. For this reason, it is important that the unbeliever have some understanding of the scope of Islamic law. Sharia is all encompassing and it is hoped that this short report will serve to illustrate just what that means for the believer and unbeliever alike.

Throughout this review I will refer to the foundational doctrine of Islam - the Koran and Hadith (stories and traditions about Mohammed); the 'Sira' (8thc biography) of Mohammed by Ibn Ishaq (1) and 'Reliance of the Traveller, a Classic Manual of Sharia Sacred Law' (ROT) written by al-Misri in the 14th Century and translated by Nuh Ha Mim Keller (2).

The ROT is derived from the foundational doctrine (as is all Islamic law) and this will be demonstrated throughout by providing examples of both. I have a 2015 Edition of the ROT (over 1200 pages) and will reference it frequently. Hadith will be identified by name of the collection such as: Bukhari, Muslim, Dawud, Ibn Majah, al-Nasa'i and Tirmidhi.

Sharia itself is the 'ordained way', of Islam which includes all the teachings found in the Koran and example of Mohammed, but because there are thousands of hadith plus the Koran to sort through the manual is a handy compendium of well established teachings. The manual is also useful to have because not all hadith have been translated (such as Musnad Ahmad – 4%) but the lessons they impart may be found in this book.

ROT Chapter Headings Include:

- SACRED KNOWLEDGE

- ZAKAT (Islamic tax) how it is spent and who can receive it (not non Muslims)

- TRADE: loans, collateral, bankruptcy, partnerships, finance, rent, endowments

- INHERITANCE: Estate division (male or female) and prevention (non Muslim)

- PURITY: Trimming fingernails and toenails, using a toothstick, circumcision, dyeing hair, dogs

- MARRIAGE: conjugal rights, defects, child custody, bride's guardian and bride price

- DIVORCE: who may effect (man), 3 pronouncements, payment for release (by wife)

- JUSTICE: retaliation & indemnity, apostasy, jihad, spoils of battle, non-Muslim subjects of Islamic state, penalties (including scourging, stoning etc.) theft, drinking, oaths and expiation for, judgeship, court claims, witnessing and testifying (1 male = 2 females)

- ENORMITIES: can relate to any of the other subjects such as not paying zakat, sodomy and lesbianism, drinking, fleeing combat in jihad

- HOLDING ONE'S TONGUE: 'slander', informing on another, permissible & obligatory lying, joking, musical instruments, keeping secrets

There are several recommendations at the beginning of the ROT, including Cairo's 'Alazar University' and the 'International Institute of Islamic Thought' which states that says that the translation is far from literal but it does not exceed the author's intent, thereby demonstrating the translators knowledge of sacred law'.   This is an important point and I'll show a few examples where content that might be disturbing for the English reader has been omitted or otherwise affected.**

Each ROT chapter addresses a separate subject. Omitting chapters that are of little interest to the non-Muslim such as 'prayer' this report will present a very broad overview of the rest, primarily to show the scope and all encompassing nature of sharia.   I'll follow the list of chapter headings so far as possible but there is considerable overlap at times (such as enormities) so some re-ordering will occur to facilitate understanding.

To begin, in Islam, all human activity – legal, moral, ethical – falls into one of five specific categories:

1. Obligatory

2. Recommended

3. Permitted

4. Discouraged

5. Forbidden

*Halal has no restrictions, Haram is specifically prohibited.

SACRED KNOWLEDGE

So exactly what is a follower of Islam required to believe? Well the Koran doesn't leave that question up to chance:

- "It is not for a believing man or a believing woman when Allah and his messenger [Mohammed] have decided a matter that they should have any choice about their Affair and whoever disobeys has strayed into clear (Koran 33:36)

- 'we put you Mohammed in an ordained way concerning the matter of religion'. (Koran 45:18)

And from Reliance of the Traveller:

- ROT a1.4 "...the good of the acts of those morally responsible is what the Lawgiver (syn Allah or His messenger) has indicated is good by permitting it or asking that it be done. And the bad is what the Lawgiver has indicated is bad by asking it not be done. The good is not what reason considers good, nor the bad what reason considers bad. The measures of good and bad... is the Sacred Law, not reason" (ROT a1.4)

- ROT p75.3 Mohammed said 'None of you believes until his 'inclinations conform to what I have brought' [this is an enormity]

It is the foundational doctrine of Islam that determines what is and what is not, halal or haram – good or bad.

- ROT a4.2 As for the basic obligation of Islam, and what relates to tenets of faith, **it is adequate for one to believe in everything brought by the Messenger of Allah** [Mohammed] and to credit it with absolute conviction free of any doubt. Whoever does this is not obliged to learn the evidences of the scholastic theologians...Rather, **what befits the common people** and vast majority of those learning or possessing Sacred Knowledge is to refrain from discussing the subtleties of scholastic theology, lest corruption difficult to eliminate find its way into their basic religious convictions.

- Whoso obeys me obeys God; and whose disobeys me disobeys God. Whoso obeys my commander obeys me, and whoso disobeys my commander disobeys me. (Muslim 1835c)

Not Conforming Can Have Serious Consequences:

It is because of sharia that people who are said to be Muslim, but do not adhere to its teachings, can be killed as apostates for leaving Islam if they are: sane, have reached puberty and voluntarily apostatize. There is no Indemnity for killing an apostate because this is like killing someone who 'deserves to die'.

- Mohammed said "The blood of a Muslim who confesses that none has the right to be worshipped but Allah and that I am His Apostle, cannot be shed except in three cases: In Qisas for murder, a married person who commits illegal sexual intercourse **and the one who reverts from Islam (apostate) and leaves the Muslims**." (Bukhari 6878)

- ROT o8.1 When a person who has reached puberty and is sane voluntarily apostatizes from Islam, he deserves to be killed.

- ROT o8.4 There is no indemnity for killing an apostate (0: or any expiation, since it is killing someone who deserves to die.)

APOSTASY

The subject of apostasy comes later in the chapter on 'Justice' but is being introduced here to illustrate that failing to adhere to the Islamic imperatives regarding 'belief' can have dire consequences for a Muslim. Many Muslims have been killed for apostasy and not only those wishing to leave Islam but also for failing to follow sharia as demanded by whoever holds authority, that could be a parent, it might be your government. Not every parent, or government enforces the doctrine to the same degree but when closely followed, as in Afghanistan, Iran and many other

Islamic countries, acting in a way considered disrespectful of Mohammed or the Koran can result in years in prison or even death.

After Mohammed's death thousands disobeyed by trying to leave Islam but were killed in the 'RIDDA' (apostasy) wars led by the first caliph Abu Bakr - they had 'no choice about their affair'.

Acts that entail leaving Islam [apostasy] include to revile Allah or Mohammed or to deny that Allah intended Mohammed's message to be the religion followed by the entire world (ROT 08.7).

- Mohammed said "I have been commanded to fight against people till they testify that there is no god but Allah, that Muhammad is the messenger of Allah..." (Muslim 22)

- "...keep firm those who have believed, I will cast fear into the hearts of those who disbelieved so **STRIKE** on the necks and upon every fingertip." (Koran 8:12)

Note that the word 'strike' is bolded, this is an example of a word being interpreted a couple of different ways. Here, the word is clearly meant to cause injury but we'll come back to it again later.

Apostasy applies to slaves as well (Dawud 4360). It is estimated that in Niger today there are 130,000 slaves and yet that portion of the ROT addressing slavery, was not translated into English. I do have the translation, but it's not in the Manual.

If a Muslim is married to someone who reverts from Islam, this is considered a defect in the spouse permitting the annulment of a marriage. A Muslim man is permitted to marry a non-Muslim woman but a Muslim woman, is not permitted to marry a non-Muslim man (Koran 2:221).

DEFECTS IN THE SPOUSE PERMITTING ANNULMENT OF MARRIAGE

ROT m7.4 If any of the following occurs before intercourse has taken place, then the marriage is immediately annulled:

(1) one of a couple who are idolators becomes a Muslim;

(2) one of a Zoroastrian couple becomes Muslim;

(3) the wife of a Jew or Christian becomes a Muslim;

(4) both husband and wife leave Islam;

(5) or one of them does.

But when one of the above situations occurs after intercourse, then a waiting period (def: n9) must intervene before the marriage is annulled. If both husband and wife (A: are, or) become Muslim before the waiting period finishes, then their marriage continues. And if not, then the marriage is considered to have been over since the change of religion first took place.

For example, if one of the partners in a non-Muslim marriage becomes a Muslim then that is considered to have ended the marriage.

Children are not exempt from this, a child of seven is ordered to pray and at 10 is beaten for not praying (Dawud 494 and ROT f1.2) and the same goes for fasting. At seven years of age they are ordered to fast and when they're 10 they are beaten for neglecting it.(ROT i1.5) To ensure Islamic principles are followed it is offensive (not forbidden) to send a child to a daycare run by non-Muslims where religion is not mentioned.

ROT m13.3 (A: It is offensive to send one's children to a day-care center run by non Muslims. It is unlawful to send Muslim children to Christian schools, or those which are designedly atheist, though it is not unlawful to send them to public schools in which religion is not mentioned (N: in a way that threatens the students' belief in Islam).)

Making up missed prayers is not just recommended, it's obligatory but "1. a Muslim who misses a prayer out of unconcern cannot by that fact alone be considered an unbeliever and 2. the view that a prayer purposely missed cannot be made up is incorrect." (ROT w18.1).

There are many examples in the hadith of making up missed prayers:

A man who slept and missed a prayer or forgot it (al-Nasa'i 614) because of business (Bukhari 7434) or as Mohammed's wife Aisha said of Mohammed himself missing a night prayer for pain or any other reason he would do make up prayers in the day time (Muslim 746e)

In 2023 it made it into Western news, that the Islamic government of Afghanistan was not allowing girls over the age of 12 to go to school. Numerous Islamic scholars came out to say that Islam does not ban a child's education. So why does Afghanistan?

It's true that the doctrine doesn't specifically ban a girl's education but the education that is obligatory in Islam is very limited. The guardian must only "train the child in points of Islamic behaviour" (ROT t3:16) and "teach the child about **purification**, prayer, fasting and so forth...". At the time of Mohammed there were no schools like we see them today so of course the foundational doctrine does not forbid girls going to them. They didn't exist and the teaching that is considered mandatory doesn't require a school.

PURIFICATION

** I mentioned earlier that the ROT translation is not literal and there are times when, if what is read in the ROT is inconsistent with what is known, it is best to double check. Below is the ROT entry for circumcision, but let's just double check the definition of 'bazr' because the Arabic (unusually) is also provided in the English definition. Of course an Arabic speaker would immediately know the correct definition but there is an English footnote saying the opposite, that this is not referring to the clitoris 'as some mistakenly assert'.

As you will see, there is a discrepancy between what the ROT has written in English, and what it says in the Arabic that has been inserted into the English translation.

PURITY

ROT e4.3 Circumcision is obligatory for both men and women.(O: for both men and women. For men it consists of removing the prepuce from the penis, and for women, removing the prepuce (Ar. bazr) of the clitoris (not the clitoris itself, as some mistakenly assert).

Brill: The Encyclopedia of Islam

bazr (A, pi. buzur) : in anatomy, the clitoris: a woman who is affected by clitorism, or is believed to be so. An uncircumcised woman is called lakhnd*. Expressions such as Ibn al-~ or Ibn al-lakhnd meaning in effect 'son of the uncircumcised woman' are considered injurious

Additionally, taking the Arabic alone from the same book (English on one side and Arabic on the other), there is no such footnote on the Arabic side of the text as you see translated below).

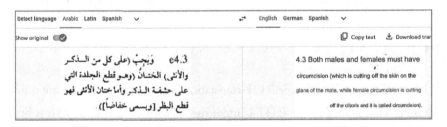

There are thousands of reports of young girls being taken from non-Islamic countries (where it's illegal) to be circumcised in Islamic countries on their school holidays or undergoing genital cutting 'behind closed doors' (3). Even though it

is often said that female circumcision is not part of Islamic doctrine, the example of Mohammed is sufficient to recommend it. From the Hadith:

It was narrated that 'Aishah the wife of the Prophet said:

- "When the two circumcised parts meet, then bath is obligatory. The Messenger of Allah and I did that, and we bathed." (Ibn Majah 608)

- And abide in your houses and do not display yourselves as [was] the display of the former times of ignorance. And establish prayer and give zakah and obey Allah and His Messenger. Allah intends only to remove from you the impurity [of sin], O people of the [Prophet's] household, and to purify you with [extensive] purification. (Koran 33:33)

Purity includes how a believer should look – and that they should not imitate the unbeliever even if they think that might be better. Unbelievers are considered 'Najasun' – impure but this word is also used elsewhere in connection with 'filth'.

THE BODY

- ROT e4.1 **It is sunna**: [in accordance with the Koran and the example of Mohammed]

  ○ (2) to clip one's mustache (0: when it grows long. The most one should clip is enough to show the pink of the upper lip. Plucking it out or shaving it off is offensive.) (A: Shaving one's beard is unlawful according to all Imams except Shafi'i, who wrote two opinions about it, one that it is offensive, and the other that it is unlawful. A weak chain of narrators ascribes an opinion of offensiveness to Imam Malik. **It is unbelief (kufr) to turn from the sunna in order to imitate nonMuslims when one believes their way to be superior to the sunna);**

- ROT e2.3 **It is offensive to use the vessels of nonMuslims**(N: before washing them) (0: **to be certain of the purity of the vessels used, since nonMuslims are not as concerned about purity as Muslims are) or wear their clothes (0: for the same reason).**

- Oh you who believe (in Allah's Oneness and in His Messenger (Muhammad)! **Verily, the** Mushrikun (polytheists, pagans, idolaters, **disbelievers** in the Oneness of Allah, and in the Message of Muhammad) are **Najasun (impure)**... (Koran 9:28)

MARRIAGE

What about the rest of the family? In Canada, when the Islamic population was still less than 5%, shelters for abused women were reporting 40% of intakes were Muslim women. Now several shelters have been built specifically for them (4). What does sharia have to say about this?

"Men are in charge of women by [right of] what Allah has given one over the other and what they spend [for maintenance] from their wealth. So righteous women are devoutly obedient... those [wives] from whom you fear arrogance - [first] advise them; [then if they persist], forsake them in bed; and [finally], strike them..." (Koran 4:34)

THE HUSBAND'S RIGHTS

- m5.4 A husband possesses full right to enjoy his wife's person (A: from the top of her head to the bottoms of her feet, though anal intercourse is absolutely unlawful) in what does not physically harm her. He is entitled to take her with him when he travels.

- m10.12 When a husband notices signs of rebelliousness in his wife whether in words, as when she answers him coldly when she used to do so politely. or he asks her to come to bed and she refuses. contrary to her usual habit; or whether in acts, as when he finds her averse to him when she was previously kind and cheerful). he warns her in words ... The warning could be to tell her, "Fear Allah concerning the rights you owe to me," or it could be to explain that rebelliousness nullifies his obligation to support her and give her a turn amongst other wives, or it could be to inform her, "Your obeying me is religiously obligatory". If she commits rebelliousness, he keeps from sleeping (0: and having sex) with her without words, and may hit her, but not in a way that injures her, meaning he may not (A: bruise her,) break bones, wound her, or cause blood to flow. (0: It is unlawful to strike another's face.) He may hit her whether she is rebellious only once or whether more than once, though a weaker opinion holds that he may not hit her unless there is repeated rebelliousness.

- (2) It is not lawful for a wife to leave the house except by the permission of her husband, though she may do so without permission when there is a pressing necessity. Nor may a wife permit anyone to enter her husband's home unless he agrees, even their unmarriageable kin. Nor may she be alone with a nonfamily-member male, under any circumstances.

- (3) It is obligatory for a wife to obey her husband as is customary in allowing him full lawful sexual enjoyment of her person...

I think at this point it's good to mention that sharia is not necessarily followed to the letter everywhere that Islam is practiced. As Islam grows stronger, for example in Afghanistan and Iran the foundational doctrine can be enforced in its entirety. This may be happening in a single home right now but later become the law of the country depending on how strong Islam is. It's a process.

So here's another example of a discrepancy. There are two on-line search engines that are quite convenient for looking up hadith. So I was searching Muslim 974b one day and noticed that it said Mohammed had 'nudged' his wife Aisha on the chest 'which she felt' when he was angry with her. Now that seemed like an odd term to be using so I double checked the same hadith with another search engine which said 'he struck me on the chest which caused me pain' (5).

So that's definitely a conflict where one translation has been 'softened' – but just to be sure I contacted an orientalist friend to check with Lane's Arabic Lexicon. Sure enough, the word used for 'strike' here means to cause pain, inflict swelling and bruising, to strike or hit violently.

This same verb is used in Koran 8:12 noted in the 'Apostasy' section which says "...I will cast fear into the hearts of those who disbelieved so **STRIKE** on the necks and upon every fingertip" and in Koran 38:44 which tells the Bible story of 'Job'. The Koran says Job struck his wife in this way, whereas the Bible story does not. According to Islam, all the prophets in the Bible were actually Muslim.

Here's an example of sharia that one might think won't affect a non-Muslim, but it does. Change rooms at recreation centres for example, or a simple visit to the doctor's office can become problematic (6).

LOOKING AT MEMBERS OF THE OPPOSITE SEX

- m2.3 It is unlawful for a man to look at a woman who is not his wife or one of his unmarriageable kin

- m2.7 It is unlawful for a woman to show any part of her body to an adolescent boy or a non-Muslim woman

DOCTORS TREATING PATIENTS OF THE OPPOSITE SEX

- m2.10 Both (0: looking and touching) are permissible for medicinal bloodletting, cupping, and medical treatment (N: when there is real need. A Muslim woman needing medical attention must be treated by a Muslim woman doctor, or if there is none, then by a non-Muslim woman doctor. If there is none, then a male Muslim doctor may treat her, while if none of the above are available, then a male non-Muslim doctor. If the doctor is of the opposite sex, her husband or an unmarriageable male relative must be present.

Of course, this originates in the foundational doctrine but it has caused problems for the medical profession in non-Islamic countries and may delay or even prevent a woman from getting the care she needs (7).

- Koran 24:30 Tell the believing men to reduce [some] of their vision and guard their private parts. That is purer for them...

- Koran 24:31 And tell the believing women to reduce [some] of their vision and guard their private parts and not expose their adornment except... to their husbands, their fathers, their husbands' fathers, their sons, their husbands' sons, their brothers etc...

Guardians are of two types; those who may compel their female charges to marry someone and those who may not. The only Guardians who may compel their charge to marry, are a virgin bride's father or her 'father's father' – meaning to marry her to a 'suitable match' without her consent. As with Mohammed's favourite wife Aisha – married when she was six and the marriage consummated when she was 9 and he was 53..

- Mohammed "engaged me when I was a girl of six (years). We went to Medina ... Then I got ill and my hair fell down. Later on my hair grew (again) and my mother, Um Ruman, came to me while I was playing in a swing with some of my girl friends. She called me, and I went to her, not knowing what she wanted to do to me... Unexpectedly Allah's Apostle came to me in the forenoon and my mother handed me over to him, and at that time I was a girl of nine years of age." (Bukhari 3894)

- ROT m3.13 Guardians are of two types, those who may compel their female charges to marry someone, and those who may not.

  ○ The only guardians who may compel their charge to marry are a virgin bride's father or father's father, compel meaning to marry her to a suitable match (def: m4) without her consent.

As a consequence, in Iran, which follow follows sharia very closely, in 2020, over 7,000 girls under the age of 14 were married in just three months. In 2022 there were 172 girls registered for marriage under the age of nine. So who may affect a divorce? That's the next chapter in the ROT (8).

DIVORCE

As already shown in the hadith, pre-pubescent girls can be married. Here, the Koran specifies the waiting period before a divorced girl or woman can be remarried.

And those who no longer expect menstruation among your women - if you doubt, then their period is three months, **and [also for] those who have not menstruated**. And for those who are pregnant, their term is until they give birth Koran 65:4).

Divorce can only be effected by the husband who can also assign an 'agent' to do this for him. He need only say 'I divorce you' three times for it to be permanent, otherwise he can take her back again. If he has divorced her three times then she must marry, and consummate the marriage, with someone else before she can remarry the first husband (Koran 2:230). If there are children, this can be very difficult for the woman whether they are in an Islamic country or not (9) and sometimes results in a 'temporary marriage' to fulfill the obligation. This has actually given rise to something called 'halala' with men selling a temporary marriage to the woman, with sex, so she can return to the first husband (10). Conversely, a woman can only obtain a divorce if her husband gives his permission.

- ROT n1.1 **Divorce is valid from any:**

   a. **husband;**

b. who is sane;

c. has reached puberty;

d. and who voluntarily effects it.

- ROT m13.4 A woman has no right to custody (A: of her child from a previous marriage) when she remarries (0: because married life will occupy her with fulfilling the rights of her husband and prevent her from tending the child

The Agent's Discretionary Power:

- ROT k17.13 It is a necessary condition that the thing 'Y is being commissioned to do is determinately known (0: to X and Y) in some respects. Thus, if X says, "I commission you to sell my property **and conduct the divorce of my wives**," his commission is valid...

INHERITANCE

The Koran gets into great detail about who can inherit what and as with all things sharia, the Koran is the highest arbiter of what is permitted.

Koran 4:12 ...And for the wives is one fourth if you leave no child. But if you leave a child, then for them is an eighth of what you leave, after any bequest you [may have] made or debt....

Now one could say the same is true for men from a wife's estate if she has one, but because sharia restricts women in ways that limits their financial opportunities and, because a man may have more than one wife, the result is quite different. For example – if there is a child, the one-eight a wife is entitled to may have to be divided amongst four women, not just one. It is also forbidden for a Muslim to leave an inheritance to an 'unbeliever' and vice versa.

ESTATE DIVISION [wives]

- ROT 16.4 If there are two, three, or four wives, they jointly receive the one-fourth or one-eighth

THE FOUR PREVENTIVES OF INHERITING AN ESTATE DIVISION SHARE

- ROT 15.2 The second preventive is being nonMuslim: a Muslim may not inherit from a nonMuslim, and a non-Muslim may not inherit from a Muslim (dis: Ll.O)

- ROT 11.0 ...it is invalid and unlawful for a non-Muslim to inherit property through estate division from a Muslim, or vice versa.

And from the Hadith:

- Mohammed said "A Muslim cannot be the heir of a disbeliever, nor can a disbeliever be the heir of a Muslim." (Bukhari 6764)

ZAKAT

Zakat is an Islamic tax of 2.5% that every Muslim is obligated to pay if they are able. Zakat is often referred to as an Islamic charity because a portion of it will go to the poor. What many people are unaware of is that there are actually eight categories for the expenditure of zakat and the seventh category is jihad. This is not some archaic application of the tax. The current Sharia Standards Accounting Manual used in today's Islamic financial transactions provides details (11).

Again, this originates with the Koran and more detail is provided in the ROT. Because it is often described as a 'charity' it is expected that the money will go only to the poor and that it makes no difference who the poor are, whether they are Muslim or not – but that is not the case.

This is also significant because all Islamic finance and trade must conform to Sharia standards, it must have a Sharia board it must follow Sharia law. Already, Islamic finance and 'halal marketing' are quite entrenched in many non-Islamic countries and utilized by non-Muslims who likely do not realize that the Islamic tax thus generated actually supports jihad against unbelievers. Canada hosts the largest 'Halal Expo' in North America every year and is currently considering providing 'Sharia mortgages' in the country's chartered banks.

- As-Sadaqat (here it means Zakat) are only for the Fuqara' (poor), and Al-Masakin (the poor) and those employed to collect (the funds); and for to attract the hearts of those who have been inclined (towards Islam); and to free the captives; and for those in debt; **and for Allah's Cause (i.e. for Mujahidun - those fighting in the holy wars),** and for the wayfarer (a traveller who is cut off from everything); a duty imposed by Allah. And Allah is All-Knower, All-Wise. (Koran 9:60)

- ROT h1.1 Zakat is obligatory:

  ○ (a) for every free Muslim

THE EIGHT CATEGORIES OF RECIPIENTS

- ROT h8.7 It is obligatory to distribute one's zakat among eight categories of recipients, one eighth of the zakat to each category.

THOSE FIGHTING FOR ALLAH

- ROT h8.17 The seventh category is those fighting for Allah, meaning people engaged in Islamic military operations for whom no salary has been allotted in the army roster (0: but who are volunteers for jihad without remuneration).

- ROT hS.24 It is not permissible to give zakat to a non Muslim, or to someone whom one is obliged to support (def: m12.1), such as a wife or family member.

JUSTICE

The obligatory character of jihad. So now we're into justice which is a large section but a very important one as it is this chapter that over the centuries has most affected non-Muslim and also Muslim populations.

Jihad is a communal obligation. Mohammed said 'he who provides the equipment for a soldier in Jihad has himself performed Jihad'. There are various ways of Performing Jihad - money and equipment and from the Hadith - Mohammed said 'I command you with five that Allah commanded me; Listen, and Obey, Jihad, Hijra (migration) and the Jamma [communal prayer]. (Tirmidhi 2863)

- Fight against those who believe not in Allah, nor in the Last Day, nor forbid that which has been forbidden by Allah and His Messenger and those who acknowledge not the religion of truth (i.e. Islam) among the people of the Scripture (Jews and Christians), until they pay the Jizyah with willing submission, and feel themselves subdued. (Koran 9:29)

THE OBLIGATORY CHARACTER OF JIHAD

ROT o9.0 JIHAD

- (0: Jihad means to war against non-Muslims and is etymologically derived from the word mujahada, signifying warfare to establish the religion. The scriptural basis for jihad... is such Koranic verses as:

    a. "Fighting is prescribed for you" (Koran 2:216)

    b. "Slay them wherever you find them" (Koran 4:89)

    c. "Fight the idolators utterly" (Koran 9:36)

- ROT o9.1 Jihad is a communal obligation. When enough people perform it to successfully accomplish it, it is no longer obligatory upon others (0: the evidence for which is [Mohammed] saying... "He who provides the equipment for a soldier in jihad has himself performed jihad,"

- ROT o9.8 The caliph (025) makes war upon Jews, Christians, and Zoroastrians (N: provided he has first invited them to enter Islam in faith and practice, and if they will not, then invited them to enter the social order of Islam by paying the Non Muslim poll tax (jizya, def: 01 L4)-which is the significance of their paying it, not the money it-self-while remaining in their ancestral religions) (0: and the war continues) until they become Muslim or else pay the non-Muslim poll tax, 'Allah has purchased from Believers their lives and their property so they fight in the cause of Allah and so they kill and are killed'.

- ROT o9.13 When a child or a woman is taken captive, they become slaves by the fact of capture, and the woman's previous marriage is immediately annulled.

There's also booty from Jihad and literally hundreds of references to these two terms 'booty' and 'spoils of war' in the Koran and Bukhari hadith. An entire chapter of the Koran is entitled 'Spoils of War' and establishes that 20% of the booty (which includes the women and other captives who may be ransomed) is for Allah and Mohammed (or the caliph). The rest of 'the spoils' are to be divided amongst those who fight. If no fighting is necessary and the people simply submit, then 100% of the tribute 'jizya' collected from the 'dhimmis' (secondary citizens who have submitted to Islam and 'feel themselves subdued' but are not Muslim) will go to Allah and Mohammed (or the caliph).

- Mohammed said, "Allah guarantees him who strives in His Cause and whose motivation for going out is nothing but Jihad in His Cause and belief in His Word, that He will admit him into Paradise (if martyred) or bring him back to his dwelling place, whence he has come out, with what he gains of reward and booty." (Bukhari 3123)

- Indeed, Allah has purchased from the believers their lives and their properties [in exchange] for that they will have Paradise. They fight in the cause of Allah , so they kill and are killed... (Koran 9:111)

- ROT o9.14 When an adult male is taken captive, the caliph (def: 025) considers the interests (0: of Islam and the Muslims) and decides between the prisoner's death, slavery, release without paying anything, or ransoming himself in exchange for money or for a Muslim captive held by the enemy. If the prisoner becomes a Muslim (0: before the caliph chooses any of the four alternatives) then he may not be killed, and one of the other three alternatives is chosen.

Legal Testimony:

Is only acceptable from a witness who is Muslim. As it says in Koran 98:6 "Indeed, they who disbelieved among the People of the Scripture and the polytheists will be in the fire of Hell, abiding eternally therein. Those are the worst of creatures."

- ROT o24.2 Legal testimony is only acceptable from a witness who:

  - (a) is free;

  - (e) is religious (0: meaning upright (024.4) (A: and Muslim), for Allah Most High says, "Let those of rectitude among you testify" (Koran 65:2), and unbelief is the vilest form of corruption, as goes without saying);

A woman's worth, which includes her testimony is only worth half that of a man. Again, this disparity has its roots in the foundational doctrine.

- Mohammed said "O women! Give alms, as I have seen that the majority of the dwellers of Hell-fire were you (women)... I have not seen anyone more deficient in intelligence and religion than you. A cautious sensible man could be led astray by some of you... **"Is not the evidence of two women equal to the witness of one man?"..."This is the deficiency in her intelligence**... (Bukhari 304)

- ROT o24.7 The testimony of the following is legally acceptable when it concerns cases involving property, or transactions dealing with property, such as sales:

    a. two men;

    b. two women and a man;

- ROT o24.8 If testimony does not concern property, such as a marriage or prescribed legal penalties then only two male witnesses may testify (A: though the Hanafi school holds that two women nd a man may testify for marriage).

Death by mistake in a deliberate injury:

- ROT o4.9 **The indemnity for the death or injury of a woman is one-half that of a man**.

Retaliation:

Retaliation is obligatory in Islam. You must retaliate (or accept 'blood-wit' – payment) against anyone who kills a human being intentionally and without right. However, there are a few exceptions that are not subject to retaliation: a Muslim for killing a non-Muslim; killing an apostate from Islam; there is no consequence against a father and mother for killing their offspring; nor is retaliation permissible to a descendant such as when a son - say his father kills his mother. There is no expiation for killing someone who has left Islam even when someone besides the caliph kills him. From the Koran:

- So whoever has assaulted you, then assault him in the same way that he has assaulted you. (Koran 2:194)

- you who have believed, prescribed for you is legal retribution for those murdered - the free for the free, the slave for the slave, and the female for the female. But **whoever overlooks from his brother anything, then there should be a suitable follow-up and payment to him** with good conduct. (Koran 2:178)

Who is subject to retaliation for injurious crimes:

- Retaliation is obligatory (A: if the person entitled wishes to take it against anyone who kills a human being purely intentionally and without right.

- 01.2 **The following are not subject to retaliation:**

    a. a Muslim for killing a non-Muslim;

    b. a Jewish or Christian subject of the Islamic state for killing an apostate from Islam because a subject of the state is under its protection, while killing an apostate from Islam is without consequences);

    c. a father or mother (or their fathers or mothers) for killing their offspring, or offspring's offspring;

    d. nor is retaliation permissible to a descendant for (A: his ancestor's) killing someone whose death would otherwise entitle the descendant to retaliate, such as when his father kills his mother.

- ROT o5.4 (0: **There is no expiation for killing someone who has left Islam**, a highwayman, or a convicted married adulterer, even when someone besides the caliph kills him.)

Theft:

Stealing: a person's right hand is amputated for theft whether he is Muslim or non-Muslim. and if he steals a second time his left foot, the third time his left hand, he steals again then his right foot. This is still happening on a regular basis today in Islamic countries, as is crucifixion (12)(13).

- As for the thief, both male and female, cut off their hands. It is the reward of their own deeds, an exemplary punishment from Allah... (Koran 5:38)

THE PENALTY FOR THEFT

- ROT o14.1 A person's right hand is amputated... whether he is a Muslim, non-Muslim subject of the Islamic state, or someone who has left Islam, when he:

  ○ has reached puberty;

  ○ is sane;

  ○ is acting voluntarily;

The status of the non-Muslim in Islam is very low and believers are frequently warned against taking them as friends 'except as a precaution' – meaning to feign friendship when it is useful. Unbelievers are considered 'corrupt' – in this way they are never innocent because of their 'disbelief'.

- you who believe! Take not as (your) Bitanah (advisors, consultants, protectors, helpers, friends, etc.) those outside your religion (pagans, Jews, Christians, and hypocrites) since **they will not fail to do their best to corrupt you.** They desire to harm you severely. Hatred has already appeared from their mouths, but what their breasts conceal is far worse.... (Koran 3:118)

- Let not believers take disbelievers as allies rather than believers. And whoever [of you] does that has nothing with Allah , **except when taking precaution against them in prudence**... (Koran 3:28)

- ROT o24.4 Corrupt (fasiq) people.

  a. has committed an enormity (0: *meaning something severely threat-ened against [disbelief] in an unequivocal text from the Koran or hadith...*)
  (A: A legally corrupt or immoral person (fasiq) is someone guilty of (1) or (2) above.)

The Penalty for Fornication or Sodomy

It doesn't matter whether these are Muslim or non-Muslim subjects of an Islamic State or someone who has left Islam. If the offender is someone who has the capacity to remain chaste, he or she is stoned to death but a pregnant woman is not stoned until she gives birth. There are many videos of such stoning available on the internet (14)(15). Lesser offences can result in beating or whipping (16).

- ROT o12.0 **THE PENALTY FOR FORNICATION OR SODOMY** ... no matter whether the person is a Muslim, non-Muslim subject of the Islamic state, or someone who has left Islam

- ROT o12.1 The legal penalty is obligatorily imposed upon anyone who fornicates or commits Sodomy

- ROT o12.2 If the offender is someone with the capacity to remain chaste, then he or she is stoned to death

- ROT o12.6 If the penalty is stoning, the offender is stoned even in severe heat or cold, and even if he has an illness from which he is expected to recover. A pregnant woman is not stoned until she gives birth and the child can suffice with the milk of another.

- Mohammed said "O Unais! Go to the wife of this (man) and if she confesses (that she has committed illegal sexual intercourse), then stone her to death." (Bukhari 2314, 2315)

ENORMITIES

Enormities are behaviours that are forbidden 'haram' such as a wife being 'rebellious' to her male guardian or husband as mentioned in the chapter on marriage.

- ROT p42.1 "...if you fear their intractability, warn them, send them from bed, or hit them..." and they should "Remain in your homes and do not display your beauty as women did in the pre-Islamic period of ignorance" (Koran 33:33)."

Not wearing approved clothing such as the hijab or burqa is also 'haram'. The doctrine demands that Muslim women wear the veil so that they will be 'recognized and not abused' which means that for women who are not so veiled they are recognized as available to be abused. This is lately being recognized as a threat to non-Muslim women in non-Islamic countries to the extent that some women are veiling themselves to avoid assault (17).

- Mohammed "tell your wives and your daughters and the women of the believers to bring down over themselves [part] of their outer garments. That is more suitable **that they will be known and not be abused...**" (Koran 33:59)

WOMEN'S OBLIGATORY CLOTHING (from f5.3)

- ROT w23.1 (A:) The nakedness ("awra) of a woman that she is forbidden to reveal differs in the Shafi'i school according to different circumstances. In the privacy of the home, her nakedness is that which is between the navel and knees. In the prayer it means everything besides the face and hands. And **when outside the home on the street, it refers to the entire body** (N: or for Hanafis, all but the face and hands, just as in prayer).

Mohammed also cursed effeminate men and masculine women and said to 'turn them out of your houses' (Bukhari 5886) which is reflected in the ROT.

MASCULINE WOMEN AND EFFEMINATE MEN

- ROT p28.1 Mohammed said:

1. The Prophet (Allah bless him and give him peace) cursed effeminate men and masculine women.

2. The Prophet (Allah bless him and give him peace) cursed men who wear women's clothing and women who wear men's.

SODOMY AND LESBIANISM

- ROT pI7.3 The Prophet (Allah bless him and give him peace) said:

    a. "Kill the one who sodomizes and the one who lets it be done to him."

    b. "May Allah curse him who does what Lot's people did."

    c. **"Lesbianism by women is adultery between them."**

ACTS THAT ENTAIL LEAVING ISLAM -

There are too many to include here but this is one example:

- ROT o8.7(20) or to deny that Allah intended the [Mohammed's] message to be the religion followed by the entire world

- Allah drew the ends of the world near one another for my sake. And I have seen its eastern and western ends. And the dominion of my Ummah would reach those ends which have been drawn near me and I have been granted the red and the white treasure... (Muslim 2889a)

Making pictures is also forbidden:

- ROT p44.1 Mohammed said:

  ○ "Every maker of pictures will go to the fire, where a being will be set upon him for each picture he made, to torment him in hell"

- ...Mohammed said ""The people who will receive the severest punishment from Allah will be the picture makers.'" (Bukhari 5950)

At this point you may be wondering why some of what your reading is contrary to what you've been told in the past – you may have believed that it didn't matter what religion you follow and that Islam was favourable towards 'people of the book' – but that's not the case. The only exception for 'people of the book' is that they might be offered the opportunity to pay 'jizya' and 'feel themselves subdued' (Koran 9:29) instead of being killed. The Koran accuses them of having 'corrupted' their scriptures because they do not accord with biblical stories as they are told in the Koran. Every word in the Koran was uttered by Mohammed. That's why knowing the life of Mohammed is so very important, the biography by Ibn Ishaq is a very good one to help put everything in context because neither the Koran, nor the Hadith, are in chronological order.

During the first 13 years of Mohammed's preaching, prior to the migration (hijra) to Medina Mohammed had only 150 followers and that period includes verses that are intolerant, but did not include violence. They are still true because they were 'revealed' to Mohammed and are said to be from Allah, but many of them have been abrogated by the later verses. An example would be from the early time in Mecca, you may have heard the saying "to you is your religion and to me is mine". But the later verses are considered better, stronger and these are the verses that non-Muslims don't ordinarily hear unless they're living in an Islamic country - but they're part of the Corpus nevertheless.

The start of the Islamic calendar begins with Mohammed's migration to Medina and it is then that Jihad was adopted. Mohammed personally took part in 27 of 65 battles to conquer the entire Arabian peninsula and consequently, the later verses are quite different (18). Because Islam is dualistic in this way it can be confusing to the non-Muslim, also because favourable doctrine applies to believer, the 'ummah' – the worldwide community of Muslims, but not to the unbeliever.

- Mohammed said, "None of you will have faith till he wishes for his (Muslim) brother what he likes for himself." (Bukhari 13)

TRADE

According to sharia, if a Koran is being purchased for someone it is obligatory that the person be Muslim. In fact non-Muslims have not really had access to Islamic Doctrine until the last couple of decades but with improved literacy, electronic communication and global migration, the situation has changed. Eighty percent of the world's Muslims don't actually speak Arabic (let alone the Classic Arabic of the original doctrine) and they're in many countries. The foundational doctrine has of necessity been translated into the language of those countries so non-Muslims have also acquired more liberal access to the texts.

The Koran states that 'none should touch it except the purified' (Koran 56:79) which does not include the non-believer.

- ROT k1.2(e) If a Koran is being purchased for someone, it is obligatory that the person be Muslim (0: The same is true of books of hadith and books containing the words and deeds of the early Muslims. "Koran" in this context means any work that contains some of the Koran, even a slight amount.).

There are some very unusual subjects included in the Trade section that you might not expect, for example dogs where 'purity' again comes up using the same word that was used earlier to describe the 'unbeliever'.

- PURITY ROT k2.2 It is invalid to transact something that is impure in itself (najasa, def: e14.1) such as a dog, or something affected with filth that cannot be purified (0: by washing), like milk or shortening, though if it can be, like a garment, then it may be transacted.

- Mohammed "ordered that the dogs should be killed." (Bukhari 3323) and said,

- "Angels do not enter a house that has either a dog or a picture in it." (Bukhari 3322)

Trade also includes adoption: it is unlawful in Islam when it means giving a child one's own name or a share of one's estate, this is found in Koran. That came about when Mohammed received a 'revelation' that he could marry his adopted son's wife after the son had divorced her. Previously, this was not acceptable.

- Allah has not made for a man two hearts in his interior. And He has not made your wives whom you declare unlawful your mothers. And he has not made your adopted sons your [true] sons... (Koran 33:4)

Reliance of the Traveller does not provide a translation for the section on slaves ROT k32.1 – instead it says that the 'issue is no longer current'. We can only wish that was true. Slavery is still very active where sharia is followed and in Niger alone, it is estimated that there are 130,000 slaves. Niger is an Islamic country (19).

Of course there is a great deal more in Trade but this gives you an example of how diverse the doctrine about trade is.

HOLDING ONE'S TONGUE

Mohammed said '...whoever conceals (the faults of) a Muslim, Allah will conceal him (his faults) in this world and the Day of Resurrection" (Ibn Majah 225). Concealing the faults of a fellow Muslim is thereby rewarded and it is an 'Enormity' to 'show others the weak points of the Muslims (ROT w52.1(384)

- ROT r2.6 The Prophet (Allah bless him and give him peace) said:

1) "The talebearer will not enter paradise." 3) "The Muslim is the brother of the Muslim. He does not betray him, lie to him, or hang back from coming to his aid. All of the Muslim is inviolable to his fellow Muslim: his reputation, his property, his blood. God fearingness is here [N: pointing to his heart]. It is sufficiently wicked for someone to belittle his fellow Muslim."

How can this be accomplished? There are not only verses about deception in the Koran, they are also in the hadith and found in the ROT. Mohammed quite famously said ""War is deceit." (Bukhari 3030) but he also said:

- "He who makes peace between the people by inventing good information or saying good things, is not a liar." (Bukhari 2692) and, from the Koran...

- Freedom from (all) obligations (is declared) from Allah and His Messenger (SAW) to those of the Mushrikun (polytheists, pagans, idolaters, disbelievers in the Oneness of Allah), with whom you made a treaty. (Koran 9:1)

'Scholars say there is no harm in giving a misleading impression if it is required by an interest countenanced by sacred law' which means that it is permitted, recommended or even obligatory.

- ROT r10.3 "Scholars say that **there is no harm in giving a misleading impression if required by an interest countenanced by Sacred Law...**"

- ROT r8.2 Outright lying is permissible in 3 cases: "war, settling disagreements, and a man talking with his wife or she with him."

- ROT r8.2 Deception, such as omitting important information to leave an erroneous impression, is preferable but **"it is permissible to lie**

when the goal is permissible... obligatory if the goal is oblig-atory." "But it is religiously more precautionary in all such cases to employ words that give a misleading impression..."

Musical Instruments

Other interesting items found in holding one's tongue that you might not expect include musical instruments – from the 'pre-Islamic period of igno-rance'. History is rife with examples where evidence of non-Islamic cultures have been destroyed for that reason (20). Mohammed particularly disliked bells and predicted that at the end times:

- '... there will be some people who will consider illegal sexual in-tercourse, the wearing of silk, the drinking of alcoholic drinks and the use of musical instruments, as lawful... Allah will destroy them during the night and will let the mountain fall on them, and He will transform the rest of them into monkeys and pigs and they will remain so till the Day of Resurrection." (Bukhari 5590)

- ROT r40.1 (1) "Allah Mighty and Majestic sent me [Mohammed] as a guidance and mercy to believers and commanded me to do away with musical instruments, flutes, strings, crucifixes, and the affair of the pre-Islamic period of ignorance."

- The bell is the musical instrument of the Satan. (Muslim 2114)

DARURA

Darura is not a section in the ROT. But it is an important Islamic principle that few non-Muslims are aware of, evidence of which is scattered here and there in both the doctrine and the ROT. The principle is this: 'necessity overcomes obligation'.

This is how many Muslims have practiced Islam in non-Islamic countries for decades with no apparent difficulty. Until recently, Islamic Finance wasn't available in non-Islamic countries. Neither was there halal marketing or prayer rooms in schools and there didn't seem to be much concern about it. This is because of the principle of darura: a dispensation made when what is normally forbidden is made permissible because of necessity or need. So if there's no Islamic Finance available then there's no problem with taking out an ordinary student loan.

Here are a few examples:

- ROT c6.2 Dispensation is when what is normally forbidden is made permissible because of necessity or need. For example, if someone is forced to make a statement of unbelief (kufr) it is made permissible, to ease his hardship, for him to do so as long as faith remains firm in his heart. one is excused an interruption if the need arises since **necessity excuses one from 'any rule whatever'** but only to the degree demanded by necessity.

When you look up 'darura' in the Brill Encyclopedia of Islam it says this:

"...in law, has a narrow meaning: what may be called the technical state of necessity... and in a wider sense, to describe **the necessities or demands of social and economic life**...The legal schools agree that prohibitions of a religious character may be disregarded in cases of necessity and danger, while **most of the offences committed under the rule of necessity are excused without any form of punishment**."

So if there's only a vegetarian lunch available that is not halal, but you're hungry and you choose to eat, that's applying the principle of Darura. The roots are in the Koran:

- He has only forbidden to you dead animals, blood, the flesh of swine, and that which has been dedicated to other than Allah . But whoever is forced [by necessity], neither desiring [it] nor transgressing [its limit] -

then indeed, Allah is Forgiving and Merciful. (Koran 16:115)

So we'll finish up here with what most people are familiar with – the Universal Code of Human Rights, which states there is freedom of religion and all are equal before the law. As you can see, that is not the case with Sharia, the 'ordained way of Islam' that we have just examined.

The Universal Code of Human Rights and Sharia are incompatible, and mutually exclusive. Something to think about when making important decisions.

Sources:

(1) The Life of Mohammed (Sira) by Ibn Ishaq

(2) Sharia manual (ROT): Reliance of the Traveller Nuh Ha Mim Keller, Amana Publications 2015 (ROT)
https://archive.org/details/relianceofthetravellertheclassicmanualofislamicsacre
dlaw

(3) Canada News:
https://www.theglobeandmail.com/opinion/article-when-will-canada-take-acti
on-for-girls-who-endure-fgm/

(4) Canada News:
https://www.cbc.ca/news/canada/calgary/muslim-domestic-violence-shelter-cal
gary-1.4948416

(5) Hadith Muslim 974b (two translations) https://sunnah.com/muslim:974
And https://quranx.com/Hadith/Muslim/USC-MSA/Book-4/Hadith-2127

(6) Arab News:
https://www.arabnews.com/news/525696

(7) British Medical Journal:
https://jme.bmj.com/content/37/1/40

(8) NCRI Women's News:
https://women.ncr-iran.org/2020/12/02/child-marriages-in-iran-over-7000-girls-under-14-got-married-in-3-months/

(9) US News:
https://www.theguardian.com/us-news/2023/sep/11/us-activist-custody-battle-saudi-arabia-bethany-alhaidari

(10) 'Halala, the men who sell divorce' BBC video:
https://www.youtube.com/watch?v=TlvNMlIMWhw

(11) 'Shari'ah Standards' The Accounting and Auditing Organization for Islamic Finance 2017, Section 35 (9) p 896
https://aaoifi.com/shariaa-standards/?lang=en

(12) Iran Wire:
https://iranwire.com/en/news/125162-iranian-mans-fingers-amputated-for-stealing-five-sheep/

(13) US Dept of Justice:
https://www.ojp.gov/ncjrs/virtual-library/abstracts/sharia-penalties-and-ways-their-implementation-kingdom-saudi-0#:~:text=Theft%20(stealing%20in%20secret)%20is,the%20severity%20of%20the%20offense

(14) Al Jazeera News:
https://www.youtube.com/watch?v=VVvD8Xe7Ngw

(15) France News:
https://www.youtube.com/watch?v=50W95eL7l3k

(16) Indonesia:
https://www.youtube.com/watch?v=y3uL-ImE3Mc

(17) Austria News: News Austria
https://theliberal.ie/austrian-mp-claims-women-in-vienna-are-wearing-veils-to
-avoid-sexual-harassment-from-muslim-men/

(18) Guillaume, Alfred. 'The Life of Muhammad: a Translation of Ishaq's Sirat
Rasul Allah' (p. 659), Oxford University Press, 1982
https://archive.org/details/GuillaumeATheLifeOfMuhammad/page/n3/mode/
2up

(19) Slavery in Africa:
https://www.theguardian.com/global-development/2022/jun/28/child-sex-traff
icking-wahaya-girls-slavery-niger

(20) NBC News:
https://www.nbcnews.com/news/world/taliban-destroyed-afghanistans-ancien
t-buddhas-now-welcoming-tourists-rcna6307

THE SOLUTION: ADDRESSING ISLAM FROM A NON-ISLAMIC PERSPECTIVE IN NON-ISLAMIC COUNTRIES

For the purpose of this report, Canada will serve as an example because I know it best. What has happened in Canada, has happened or is happening in non-Islamic countries right around the globe whether we're speaking of the European Union, the United Kingdom, Australia, the United States or elsewhere – the story is the same, so too are the solutions.

BACKGROUND: Historically, Canada has enjoyed a global reputation as a champion of human rights, and a safe haven for those suffering overt discrimination and abuse in their countries of origin – to the point of genocide – owing to their religious beliefs or immutable characteristics. This is no longer the case. People who came to this country seeking safety and a better life – not just in recent decades but historically as well – recognize harbingers of former oppression now in Canada – signs that the average Canadian has little experience with or knowledge of and fails to see. Ultimately this failure will negatively impact not only Canada's reputation, but the well-being and security of its entire population.

DISCUSSION: Islamic law, which is the Koran and Hadith (words and actions of Mohammed) in practice, does not permit freedom of religion or equality before the law. In this way, the Cairo Declaration – subscribed to by Islamic states

– is the antithesis of the Universal Declaration of Human Rights underpinning Canadian society. Islamic law is inseparable from the practice of Islam, this is the fundamental doctrine (Koran 45:18). When it is closely followed by a country, we recognize it – Afghanistan, Iran, Saudi Arabia – when it happens in someone's home, or slowly enters our society we do not.

While it's true that many Muslims came to Canada to enjoy more freedom than they did in their home country, there is also an imperative to spread Islam globally. We see this very clearly in the UK where there are over 85 Sharia courts where a woman's testimony is worth half that of a man's (1)(2). This is in spite of concerns expressed in an EU Parliamentary Assembly report that sharia clearly discriminates against women:

"8. The Assembly is also concerned about the "judicial" activities of "Sharia councils" in the United Kingdom. Although they are not considered part of the British legal system, Sharia councils attempt to provide a form of alternative dispute resolution, whereby members of the Muslim community, sometimes voluntarily, often under considerable social pressure, accept their religious jurisdiction mainly in marital issues and Islamic divorce proceedings but also in matters relating to inheritance and Islamic commercial contracts. **The Assembly is concerned that the rulings of the Sharia councils clearly discriminate against women in divorce and inheritance cases. The Assembly is aware that informal Islamic courts may also exist in other Council of Europe member States**" (3).

Additionally, in European countries women are being urged to veil themselves even though they are not Muslim in order to avoid attack (4). This is a matter of national security for non-Muslim women arising from the Koranic requirement for Muslim women to cover themselves so they will be '**known and not be abuse**.' (Koran 33:59)

Polygynous marriages (5)(6) and pressure to conform to other forms of sharia such as Islamic finance and halal certification only increase when non-Islamic countries accommodate demands that would never be tolerated in an Islamic country were the roles reversed. Even now in Canada, it is impossible to purchase non-halal gelatin capsules. This has a negative impact on not only the pork industry in general but ultimately affects employment as well (7). Islamic finance requires that there be a 'Sharia board' that will follow Sharia Accounting Standards including a mandatory payment of an Islamic tax called 'zakat' (8). There are eight categories for the expenditure of zakat, one of which is jihad. (Koran 9:60, 9:29). Jihad takes many forms, money, gifts, violence and activism which is already highly organized and advanced in Canada.

There are legitimate and concrete steps that non-Islamic countries can take to resist and even reverse Islamisation but it requires knowledge from the non-Islamic perspective. When our educational system, governments or judiciary* (9) call upon Islamic organizations for advice, they are contributing to the Islamisation of Canada because it is 'haram' – forbidden – for Muslims to assist a non-believer to the detriment of Islam. It's unrealistic to expect otherwise (Koran 48:29). In fact, it is not uncommon for non-Muslim experts to be derided (knowingly or unknowingly) instead of appreciating that their knowledge of Islam, from the perspective of the non-Muslim is exactly the approach that a non-Islamic country should be taking. Even the voices of those who have themselves suffered under Islamic regimes or apostatized are silenced as 'Islamophobes' (10).

Currently, host countries continue to disregard the significance of Mohammed and the imperative for advocates to foster sympathy and support for Islam. For example, in 2023 Canada's 'Special Representative on Combatting Islamophobia' reported to senate that there had been a 71% rise in hate crimes against Muslims. She neglected to mention that those same statistics showed that Jews were 18X more likely to be targeted than Muslims, and there had been a 260% increase against Catholics over the same period (11). In the following year hate crimes against the Jewish population continued to rise and in fact doubled (12).

The use of deception is permitted if the sharia goal is permitted and obligatory if the goal is obligatory (13).

Mohammed said "Indeed Allah gathered the earth for me so that I saw its east and its west. And surely my Ummah's authority shall reach over all that was shown to me of it..."

RECOMMENDATIONS:

1. That education at every level (including the judiciary) be from a non-Islamic perspective recognizing that more than half of the Koran consists of Koranic arguments against the non-believer and how they should be treated. They are the "...worst of creatures" (Koran 98:6)

2. Acknowledge the significance of Mohammed, the Islamic imperative to follow his example and the consequent dual nature of Islam. Early doctrine is intolerant but not violent, later doctrine, reflecting Mohammed's transformation to politician and military leader marks the beginning of the Islamic calendar and is violent. Analyze Mohammed's strategies and tactics because they are still employed today – the three stages of jihad.

"He who obeys the messenger has obeyed Allah..." (Koran 4:80)

3. Utilize the Islamic principle of 'darura' – 'necessity overcomes obligation' or 'necessity makes the forbidden permissible' rather than accommodating ongoing demands for sharia compliance, whether at a recreation centre or prayer rooms in a school. There is no 'wrong doing', for example, using traditional student loans or eating non-halal food if sharia compliant alternatives are not available. Make up prayers can be said later (Bukhari 7434) (14).

4. Recognize that it is 'haram' (forbidden) for proponents of Islam to reveal information to a non-Muslim that would be detrimental to another Muslim or Islam and the threat this poses to the judicial system:

"Scholars say that there is no harm in giving a misleading impression if required by an interest countenanced by Sacred Law..."(15).

5. Utilize concise language. Fuzzy language creates fuzzy thinking. Jihad, hijra (migration), zakat (not charity). Forensic linguistics pertaining to Islam and its dualistic nature attest to the need for this.

6. Adding the study of Islam to the curriculum of University Political Science departments – dualistic and expansive – from the non-Islamic perspective of those populations that have been oppressed and conquered by Islam. Similarly, in Religious Studies, Islam should always be taught from the perspective of the non-Muslim in non-Islamic states. Teaching from an Islamic perspective will inevitably result in the Islamization of the student body.

7. Acknowledge that Islamic doctrine does not recognize freedom of religion and equality before the law (as per the 2021 Cairo Declaration), and on that basis, restrict or prohibit charitable status, foreign funding, government grants etc. to organizations that promote sharia. Sharia is simply the ordained way of Islam and is therefore inherent to the practice of Islam.

8. Phase out Islamic finance with the concomitant Sharia boards that support sharia and collect zakat which can directly or indirectly finance jihad.

9. Polygamy: At a minimum: require ALL Imams to register every marriage that they perform with the government to prevent 'Imam shopping' to accommodate 2nd - 3rd and 4th marriages.

10. Islamic schools (madrasas) and mosques utilize one of the two official languages for teaching and sermons with an exception made for teaching language.

Sources:

(1) UK House of Commons:
https://researchbriefings.files.parliament.uk/documents/CDP-2019-0102/CDP-2019-0102.pdf

(2) UK Hansard:
https://hansard.parliament.uk/commons/2019-05-02/debates/201F2DB0-FCE5-412F-AAB8-83CAA66F308A/ShariaLawCourts

(3) EU Parliamentary Assembly #8:
https://assembly.coe.int/nw/xml/XRef/Xref-XML2HTML-en.asp?fileid=25353

(4) Former Austrian MP Franz:
https://sovereignnations.com/2019/02/21/european-girls-vienna-headscarves-assaults-muslim-migrants/

(5) Video: Muslim polygamy and welfare fraud rampant in Germany:
https://www.bitchute.com/video/Wn964C49ZNcu/

(6) Polygamy in the U.K.:
http://www.gees.org/articulos/britain-muslim-polygamists-to-get-more-welfare-benefits

(7) Solomon, Sal "Islamisation through halal products" 2019
https://archive.christianconcern.com/sites/default/files/20190114_ChristianConcern_PolicyReport_HalalFoods.pdf

(8) 'Shari'ah Standards' The Accounting and Auditing Organization for Islamic Finance 2017, 'Zakah' Section 35 (9) p 896
https://aaoifi.com/shariaa-standards/?lang=en

(9) *Fatah, Tarek, Toronto Sun June 22, 2019
https://torontosun.com/opinion/columnists/fatah-shariah-law-makes-a-comeback-in-ontario

"The Ontario Superior Court judge relied on testimony by an overseas expert named Abdel Qader Thomas who appeared via video to educate the court about Islamic financial products, and who Justice Ferguson credited for educating her about Islamic banking terminology.

In her judgement, Justice Ferguson writes: "I initially believed that an unwillingness to pay conventional interest on a loan appears "bizarre" **until I learned that the payment of interest is considered a serious sin in the Islamic faith and violates a central pillar of Shariah law**. This understanding was essential in my understanding of Kalair's operating mind. Thomas' evidence was also educative regarding industry standards against which Kalair's conduct must be assessed."

Justice Ferguson shared facets of Islamic culture that she picked up in what she referred to as her "steep learning curve."

(10) ISIS survivor silenced:
https://nypost.com/2021/11/27/toronto-school-cancels-isis-survivor-event-with-nadia-murad/

(11) Stats Canada:
https://www150.statcan.gc.ca/n1/daily-quotidien/230322/cg-a004-eng.htm

(12) CBC News:
https://www.cbc.ca/news/politics/bnai-brith-antisemitic-report-record-high
-1.7195197

(13) EDUCATIONAL VIDEO: Deception in Islam
https://www.youtube.com/watch?v=9eP8tnQEWf8

(14) Sharia, Reliance of the Traveller (f2.7), Nuh Ha Mim Keller, Amana Publications 2015
https://archive.org/details/relianceofthetravellertheclassicmanualofislamicsacre
dlaw

(15) Ibid (r8.2, r10.2-3)

RELEVANT DOCTRINE

Koran 4:80 https://legacy.quran.com/4/80

Koran 9:29 https://legacy.quran.com/9/29

Koran 9:60 https://legacy.quran.com/9/60

Koran 33:59 https://legacy.quran.com/33/59

Koran 45:18 https://legacy.quran.com/45/18

Koran 48:29 https://legacy.quran.com/48/29

Hadith (Muslim 22) https://sunnah.com/muslim:22

Hadith (Muslim 2889a) https://sunnah.com/muslim:2889a

Hadith (Bukhari 2783) https://sunnah.com/bukhari/56/2

ABOUT THE AUTHOR

Ms Ellinger's interest in Islam began in 1983 owing to a chance encounter with a Bahai refugee who fled Iran during the revolution. At that time Ms Ellinger was working as a child protection Social Worker in Canada and could hardly conceive of the torture and abuse of Iranian minorities who were not Islamic and others who opposed the strict sharia that had been imposed. Since that time she has spent many years researching, writing and speaking about the growing influence of sharia – the ordained way of Islam – in non-Islamic countries.

Formerly Canadian Director for the Center for the Study of Political Islam International, she founded the 'Perspectives on Islam Society' in 2023 for the express purpose of providing public education on the foundational doctrine of Islam in the context of current events. Historically, Canada has enjoyed a reputation as a tolerant country providing safe haven for those escaping Islamic regimes and sharia. That reputation is now in jeopardy as proponents of the belief system that oppressed unbelievers and other minority groups in Islamic states have followed them to Canada and demands to accommodate sharia are regularly pressed for in this diverse and welcoming country as in others.

For the sake of future generations both here and abroad, the time for all to learn the facts about sharia and Islamic doctrine is now.

Made in the USA
Monee, IL
12 September 2024

65507541R00134